Dent in the Universe

Uncover Your Gift and Create
a Life of Significance

NORA PAXTON

Dent in the Universe

Copyright © 2024, Nora Paxton

Published by:
Thought Leader Press
New York / Oklahoma

Hardcover 978-1-61343-160-3

Paperback 978-1-61343-161-0

E-book 978-1-61343-162-7

"We're here to put a dent in the universe. Otherwise, why else even be here?"

– Steve Jobs

TABLE OF CONTENTS

Introduction

We all have a gift that has been given to us at birth. It is up to us to figure out what that gift is.

Without knowing that gift, we have no purpose on this planet. We are just passing through.

However, we do have a purpose for being on this planet. We all have a role to play, and the unique gift we each possess will help us make a mark.

The gift will help us make that dent in the universe so that our lives are not in vain.

The fact that I could die without leaving a mark is something I just can't accept.

That's why I'm here: to shake people and wake them up to the greatness that lies within. Especially those who have been dormant for so many years, leaving so much of their untapped goodness on the table. Things they've buried because of their circumstances or because they've been told to do so.

I cannot let that happen.

I'm here to help you discover your gift.

I'm here to help you break free, because I've experienced this myself.

I've been through this journey. I understand.

I personally understand how liberating it feels when you reach that point where you end up saying, "I finally found my purpose! I know my Why!"

I found mine at the age of 42, and it has been an incredible 8-year journey for me since.

I'm still feeling more fulfilled every time I help someone. I feel like it makes me stronger, and my dent is getting bigger each time.

That's why I'm here. I'm here to shake those souls.

To shake your soul.

I'm here to shake everyone reading this because we're not meant just to pass through. We're meant to make a dent in the universe.

So, let me help you do that.

My story began with the influence of many people in my life. It started with my grandpa.

I loved my grandpa. He was a very strong man with a great sense of humor. He didn't really take life seriously, but he was driven, and did everything with sarcasm and jokes. He was awesome and funny, and he loved tricking people. He just gave me so much joy, and I always looked forward to seeing him.

Unfortunately, my grandpa passed away when I

was 18. But I recognize his great influence on me. I think I got some of his sense of humor and fun, and now I appreciate and gravitate toward that.

My dad was loving, engaging, and happy when my mom was not around. As much as I could, I was able to breathe in that joy and fun and love with him, as well.

Unfortunately, I didn't get to take advantage of it too much because my parents were usually together. And as a result, he taught me both with his joy, but also his sadness.

His sadness was that he could not fulfill his dreams because he had gotten married and had children, and his wife (my mother) was often an unkind person to him, and he played second fiddle to her in so many ways.

This made me realize that I needed to do something important with my life. I didn't want to repeat the same sacrifices he made. In a way, I think he gave me a hint on the direction I needed to take.

My mom was a strong, resilient woman. I think

I got those positive traits from her, and they have helped me push through this journey. My strength, my resilience, and the fact that I am not a quitter, I got all that from her despite some of the more problematic parts of her character.

All of these people have really marked my life. In a way, they all contribute to a part of my personality and drive. I wanted to have the fun and joy of my grandpa. My father's deep sacrifices showed me that I didn't want to make similar sacrifices. The strength and resilience that my mom had was where I got the drive that I needed to push through.

However, what I didn't mention above is what I didn't enjoy about my childhood. I had a grandmother who didn't really connect with me, and a mother who was narcissistic and abusive.

I had to find myself. Why? Because I spent much of my young life constructing a protective shell to guard against all the negativity and abuse.

At some point (recently), I realized that I needed to break through that shell in order to feel completely centered in who I am and my true identity.

Through this process, I discovered my gift, the one I'm discussing with you today. This gift of finding your purpose and being able to look at yourself in the mirror and be excited by what you see.

This is where you come in, dear reader.

Just like the clients I work with every day, to break through their shell and discover their gift, I want to take you through my learnings and my experiences, and help you think about your own journey.

By experiencing a shock, your shell can be broken. You can do that by hitting a wall, or it could be done with the help of someone like me.

If you go on this journey, I can guarantee you will never be the same.

You will be happier than ever before at the end of this journey. There is no greater joy than finding that.

Wake up.

You can't just let your life pass you by without

doing anything about it. That doesn't make sense.

Why are we on this planet? Is it just to be born, eat, go to work, and go to bed?

People who think like that have no joy. They are just like robots without purpose or direction and don't make a difference.

The only way to make a difference is to discover the gift you were born with and use it.

You can make a difference in your life, the life of others, and the planet overall, because you're a piece of the puzzle.

You have to find out which piece you are and where to put it, so you can be a catalyst for more growth.

Our mess is our message.

We have to break free from our shell because that shell is our mess.

It's the false identity we have built over time that prevents us from seeing our greatness.

We have to free ourselves to see the light.

Then we can tap into our greatness and look inside ourselves ...

... to see how beautiful we are, what our unique gift is, and how to use it.

I've been put on this earth to help you make a dent in the universe.

I was put on this earth to show you how great you are, how beautiful you are, and the gift you are meant to share.

I was put on this earth to help you find fulfill-ment, to touch other people's lives as a result, and make an impact in this world.

My gift is to be the person who will say, "No, you can't give up. We're almost there!"

My gift is to help you get to the finish line, and I will never stop trying to help people until my last breath.

Our journey is never done.

We are continuously growing. You can see how many centuries of growth humanity has gone through.

It's because we never stop.

We're thirsty, and the more we discover, the more we get excited and want to continue growing.

We want to explore, and that curiosity is going to be what will bring you out of your shell. It's what's going to get you started in this process.

You were meant to play a role on this planet, to help make a difference, and to help it thrive. I don't know what it is, but I'm going to help you to figure it out if you allow me to.

If you want to take this journey by my side, I will help you find out why you are here. Because if you're reading this, it means that you don't know why.

If you knew your purpose, you would not be reading this. You would be out there practicing and sharing your gift.

I can guarantee you this: If you come on this journey with me, you will never be the same, and it will be amazing.

The other side is incredible fulfillment, joy, confidence, and love for yourself.

You will see yourself so differently.

You will learn that you were holding on to the wrong things in this world.

The temporary joys you sought out were just band-aids covering up what you really needed: this gift already inside of you.

The world I'd like to take you to is your world, a world where you're making an impact. A world where you don't need anything except this gift you inherited that is already within you.

This gift will give you constant joy and fulfillment.

You won't need other people to tell you what to do.

You won't need external things and validation

to move forward. It will be a permanent thing within you.

Even if you have a little taste of it, you will want more. It's like this little sweetness that you get access to, and you think, "This is really good. I want more of that. I like the feeling of the sun on my face. I didn't know I was in this darkness for so long."

The more you want, the more you'll go after it.

At some point, you will reach that place where you will realize you have your engine.

You can keep going and never look back.

Your gift has a stamp.

With that stamp, you dent the universe, and that dent comes with a ripple effect.

Vibrate the universe with your stamp. You will bless the universe with your gift.

What do you want people to say when you die? Do you want people to say, "Oh, he was a nice guy"? Or do you want them to say, "He changed the world around us, and he helped so many people. He created a space for us to really grow"?

If you're here just to navigate through life and not make a mark, only to be remembered as a "nice guy," then don't read this book.

However, read this book if you want to discover how amazing you are, the gift you have inherited, and how to make a difference in this world.

– Nora Paxton, February 2024

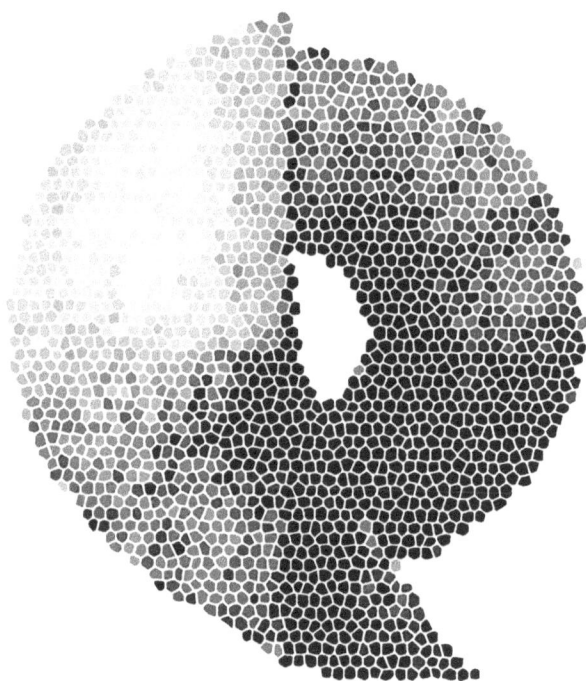

chapter one

Shell

As humans, we inadvertently layer discomfort onto ourselves by constructing a shell around our life and work.

What feels at first like a protective shell actually really holds us captive. And we need to break free.

The initial step involves identifying the very shell that holds you captive and making a resolute decision to liberate yourself from its grasp.

It is within the confines of the shell that growth is suppressed and freedom is restricted.

That feeling of "being stuck" is the signal that you're in a shell.

At the age of 25, I hit a wall.

The men I chose to date possessed an unnerving commonality. They all had a pronounced tendency toward narcissism, an inclination that also brought out the worst in me.

Their presence in my life became a source of endless misery, and I became unrecognizable even to myself.

I didn't know it at the time, but these experiences triggered haunting memories. I couldn't connect the dots with my parents yet, but I knew something was wrong.

When we first started dating, these men would put me up on a pedestal. However, it wasn't long before the dynamic shifted dramatically.

These same men soon subjected me to relentless belittlement and attempted to trap me in their own misery.

Their pain became an invitation for me to join them, to serve as their savior, as if their salvation would somehow mirror my own.

I wanted to help them, but instead, I would get burned.

I saw the patterns. This guy resembled the previous one, and so did the next.

Now, don't get me wrong. It's not like I went through a roster of 10,000 men. In fact, it was just three, but they all shared these striking similarities.

I remember telling myself, "There's something wrong."

It came to a point where I had just grown weary of the pain. It hurt the same way every time, and carrying that pain became heavier.

I needed to understand the underlying cause and the problem within myself. The fact that I kept gravitating toward the same type of person in my relationships meant I would continue hitting that wall unless I figured this out.

I began my search for a therapist. I was determined to find someone who would go beyond superficial conversations, someone capable of diving deep into the core of my being.

I did some research, and I found someone specializing in childhood trauma.

I was scared of what she would be able to pull out of me. The uncertainty and unfamiliarity with the process added to my fears. But the sheer weight of the unrelenting pain and fatigue propelled me to move forward with it.

My heart was bleeding from the scars of abandonment and a profound belief that I was unworthy of love.

We humans are interesting. Despite the difficult upbringing you might have had to endure with your parents, you still want to love them.

This complex dynamic can lead individuals who have been abused to seek out further instances of mistreatment. By associating abuse with love in their minds, they pursue partners who embody the role of the abuser.

For example, if a mother mistreats her child, yet a deep-seated belief in the mother's love persists, the association between abuse and love becomes firmly established.

It was only through the therapeutic process that this profound insight came to light.

I was scared for many reasons. I trembled at the prospect of confronting my inner demons while wrestling with the fear that my personal growth might hurt my mom.

I found myself grappling with a flicker of uncertainty: was my mom, in fact, a good mother? It triggered a period of doubt where I didn't want to hurt her because there were still some emotional dependencies.

I sought help from a psychotherapist who used a unique approach. She basically lays you down on a couch and lets your body do the talking. Without physical contact, she skillfully guided me to vocalize my experiences. This is the kind of therapeutic method they use to try to get you to talk about the abuse.

It felt like sharp pain coming out of my body, like knives piercing me.

All the pain was excruciating. It was as if actual things were physically coming out of my body.

Accompanied by tears and sobbing, the physical sensation was profound. It was a visceral reminder that our body has memories and remembers the pain.

It remembers everything.

I experienced a growing sense of liberation and clarity as the sessions progressed. I realized that what my mother had shown me was not love, even though she may have perceived it as such.

I severed the association of abuse with love. This was one of the best things I did, and the result is that I can now talk about it without crying. I used to be very emotional when talking about the abuse, but it felt like the pain had been released from my being.

The therapy sessions lasted only a year, and the therapist said that what saved me was my resilience, and the hard work I did towards awareness and relentless introspection. The very act of questioning and scrutinizing these experiences had acted as a safeguard. She acknowledged that the outcome could have been worse, with the potential for additional mental challenges or afflictions.

As a person, I have this strong ability to absorb a lot from people. This made me have a genuine fascination with understanding psychology and behaviors.

During my therapy, my therapist discussed various topics about beliefs and physical trauma and how they impact our behavior and our choices. It piqued my curiosity, and I started to read books and explore the dynamics of the father-child relationship, in particular. I focused on the father, because an imbalance in parenting, where the mother dominates, can affect the child.

This research gave me more light and clarity in my journey of healing from abuse. I gained greater insight into my experiences and the knowledge I acquired during therapy. I learned how I had connected abuse with love and normalized my father's absence while my mother took control.

However, therapy opened my eyes and relieved me from that pain. I began to see the world very differently. As I did my additional reading, I also realized that I only focused on my mom and never really paid attention to my dad.

I thought my dad was just a passive person. He didn't want to break the marriage and lose his kids, so he just stayed quiet. He just did whatever she wanted to do. At least, that was my interpretation.

Furthermore, the therapy broke down one of the barriers I had built, the belief that I was unimportant and unloved, and granted me newfound freedom. I felt better.

Seven years later, I met someone vastly different from the men I had previously dated. Eventually, he became my husband. I was feeling happier, but most importantly, I was feeling better because I had established stronger boundaries with my mother.

He lived in America, and I lived in France. After two years of dating, we decided to get married, so I moved there. I became pregnant, and he already had three children from a previous relationship. I had to navigate these dynamics while adapting to a new culture and seeking new employment. It definitely tested my resilience.

Then, around the five-year mark, I began to sense something was not right. I remember the day very clearly. We had a bad argument, we were fighting, and I yelled. And I hated yelling because I didn't want to be my mom. However, my husband's stoic response triggered a revelation: "Oh my God, he's my dad. It's like me and my dad." In that frozen moment, I stepped outside myself and observed the scene, recognizing the underlying dynamic.

I went to my room. I was extremely upset, and I had to calm myself down and try to figure out what was happening.

That's when I said, "We need to see a therapist."

I wasn't thinking about divorce or separation. I was determined to work through our issues.

Despite attempting therapy with two different professionals, we made limited progress. The fights persisted and worsened. And not only was it getting worse, but I noticed that I was losing my inner radiance.

When I ask people about me as a child or see pictures of myself, I'm actually a little ray of sunshine. But now I had lost it again.

I thought I had been getting better. And not only had I lost my radiance, but I felt like I had become a monster.

I literally thought, "I'm a monster, I'm horrible, I don't like yelling, but I'm yelling, and I'm doing all these things I hate."

During therapy, a realization struck me. Not only had I lost my inner radiance, but I had become a reflection of my mom, while my partner embodied my dad's traits. This discovery consumed me. As a result, I started taking more courses and trying to understand myself.

In our last session together, the therapist discussed the power of belief, allowing me to identify my partner's protective barrier. I was telling him, "You have this shell. I am my mom, and this is what needs to change."

But he wouldn't believe me. He wouldn't believe that he had this "shell".

Personally, I found this therapist's approach to be overly didactic, resembling a professor more than a therapist. However, I valued the knowledge I gained from those sessions, perceiving them as opportunities for continuous learning. It was not therapy for me, it was just learning.

I delved into the concept of "emotional schemas" and failed to apply it to myself. But I became well-versed in these topics, which ultimately helped me identify my partner's protective shell. Even the therapist said, "Yes, that's his shell." Despite our best efforts, our journey eventually ended in divorce.

Following the divorce, I entered a new relationship where I experienced a different kind of pain: abandonment.

I realized that as soon as my new partner encountered a problem in his own life, he ran away. Even though the relationship was very short, it had enough impact on me that I had to look into it.

I started reading some books on emotional schemas. I needed to figure out what this new shell was. What is this shell that I have?

Because now I know I have another layer, or another shell I need to break through.

When I did an assessment in one of the books I had, I learned that this shell was about abandonment. So I started to ponder on it.

Who had abandoned me?

That's when I connected it to my dad.

In many ways, my dad abandoned me. Every time my mom was abusive, he never intervened. He didn't put himself in the middle to say, "No, stop this." He would just tell us to apologize to our mom.

That was an abandonment.

He was actually very kind to us, but as soon as my mom was there, he would tell her everything that we shared privately with him. This triggered my mom to get mad at us. It was a betrayal of trust.

Another significant event during my childhood was when I was five or six years old. My mom had a prolonged absence due to open-heart surgery. It deeply impacted my sense of abandonment. For unknown reasons, I held on to this experience and was attached to it.

Meditation and research on abandonment allowed these memories to resurface. I embarked on a journey to revisit the past. I was trying to go back as far in time as I could, and I found that shell.

From there, it took me about a year to get out of it because I had to work through the memories. I wrote heartfelt letters to my parents, releasing everything I had held inside: memories, hurt, and grievances. It was a cathartic experience that offered a sense of liberation. I also wrote a letter to my younger self, reassuring her that she would be okay and thrive.

So, what do we do with our shells? How do we think about identifying them, breaking through them, and moving on?

A New Angle

First, we need to think about where we are "stuck", and where those shells are trapping us.

For example, I had the realization that I was trapped in a cycle of toxic relationships.

I was stuck in a pattern of dating narcissistic individuals who caused me harm.

I knew I could no longer endure this kind of pain, and I knew I needed help. Something had to change.

You're probably experiencing intense pain right now and feeling trapped, but I want you to know that you have a choice.

Despite feeling trapped, you still have a power you can wield that exists within you – the power to make a decision.

You can either break free from the grip of this suffering, experience a profound sense of liberation, and access your inner light, or you can choose to remain in this pain because you think things will get better.

But they won't get better. Not until you decide to confront the real issues.

In fact, continuing on this path is a downward spiral, and they will keep getting worse.

You may occasionally experience temporary relief, but there will never be any real improvement in your circumstances.

On the other hand, if you choose to free yourself from this pain, you can embark on a transformative journey of self-discovery, exploring the vast potential of what's out there for you. It's just waiting for you to break free.

Have you ever experienced that feeling of repeatedly hitting an impenetrable wall? It's the feeling of being completely stuck, unable to progress.

You look around, only to find no door, just an imposing, thick, and painful barrier. You can keep pounding away at it, hoping that it will eventually give way, or you can recognize that something is wrong and approach your situation from a different perspective.

And that's when the magic can happen.

The once formidable barrier will take on a different appearance ... if you look at it from a new angle.

That is when the shell starts to seem breakable.

Done with Pain

I've reached a point where I'm absolutely done with this pain. I'm done with feeling stuck.

It's no longer serving any purpose in my life. It's not leading me anywhere; I'm still stuck in the same place.

Except I'm actually feeling more bruised.

I want to feel joy. I'm a naturally joyful person,

and I love the feeling of happiness. I love the feeling of freedom.

It is an agonizing experience to keep continuously hitting a wall. I can choose to keep hitting that wall, but ultimately, I will only end up breaking myself and bringing myself to the end of my life faster.

There's an alternative. I can choose to live a life filled with purpose, joy, freedom, and impact.

If you continue doing nothing and keep slamming into that wall, the inevitable outcome is a life consumed by pain.

Not only that, but you are robbing yourself of the opportunity to discover your true greatness.

Imagine yourself banging into that wall over and over again. What a waste of your precious time. Do you want to squander your life like that when you have the opportunity to make a difference?

As long as you have the power to choose, you can make a difference. You have the power to create a positive, lasting impact if you choose to, and I hope you will choose that freedom.

I am here to shake you up. This is your wake-up call.

I'm here to jolt you into understanding that you're wasting the life bestowed upon you. You're allowing this precious gift to go to waste.

Will you allow it to be buried with you, forgotten and lost?

Or do you yearn to live an extraordinary life of freedom? A life where you can be authentically yourself, make a meaningful difference, and experience pure fulfillment and joy?

The choice is yours to make.

Never Coming Back

Once you have experienced the depths of suffering, the last thing you want is to return to that state. You need to keep breaking that shell. Let that memory of pain be what keeps you going.

The only thing that kept me going was the memory of that unbearable pain. It was an excruciating experience that fueled my determination to never return to it. And not only do I want to spare myself, but also anyone else, from enduring such agony.

Pleasure, fulfillment, and joy are attainable. They are innate aspects of who we are and inherent in our very DNA. While others may attempt to rob us of these qualities, they are an integral part of who we are.

You have just as much right and opportunity to experience this profound fulfillment as anyone else.

And if you still feel the inclination to return to pain, something is seriously wrong. I strongly urge you to seek help from a mental health professional as soon as possible.

Fuck, I'm My Mother

When I realized I was turning into my mom, it was horrible.

At that moment, I despised and hated myself. Though I forgiven her now and moved on, I simply couldn't stand her back then. The mere thought of her angry face brought back all the pain I had experienced. It was an instant trigger for me. Was this me now?

No, it wasn't. I was not her.

As soon as I recognized the similarity between my actions and those of my mom, I took immediate action in my life.

When people realize that they have reached rock bottom and the only direction left is up, a sense of readiness arises.

Being at rock bottom often signifies a lack of knowledge on how to initiate an upward movement. People find themselves trapped in a pit of despair, unsure how to escape.

You can use that sense of despair to cultivate your desire to break free.

I understand that sometimes you're desperate to seek help and guidance from someone that can figure it out for you. But, although I can show you how to get out, the choice to take action is entirely up to you.

Often, we don't realize that it's the self-imposed barriers that keep us confined. We unknowingly add layer upon layer to this restrictive shell, making it heavier and even more difficult to get out.

Again, when you reach rock bottom, you cannot go any lower.

Now you have a choice: remain at the bottom or shatter the shell that holds you captive.

And ascend.

If you're reading this book, I believe you're ready to rise.

There's Something More

When I talk to my clients, I emphasize the power of imagination.

The word "imagine" has power. Asking someone

to "imagine" triggers their thoughts and helps them envision a different reality.

So, to break out of your shell, you must have a vision and a desire. I can help you create a vivid picture of what your life would feel like once you escape your current circumstances and reach the pinnacle of fulfillment.

I encourage you to envision a life where you no longer have to deal with your struggles, a life where you excel in your career and experience emotional and physical fulfillment.

Are you doing that?

Now, describe what a life of fulfillment would look like for you. I hope this will force you to confront your deepest desires and aspirations.

As you articulate your vision, you gradually feel uplifted and can begin the process of breaking your shell.

Imagination always serves as the starting point. By asking my clients to imagine their ideal life and describe a state of fulfillment, I am helping them lay the foundation for transformation. I also try to explain the concept of fulfillment, that remarkable feeling of being able to breathe freely without stress.

There is always a way out, even in the face of formidable walls of pain. It lies in the choice before you. You can either view it as an impenetrable barrier or adopt a different perspective.

There is a reality in front of you, hidden by the veil of your present suffering. This reality holds a brightness far greater than it initially appears. Only those who desire to transform their pain into joy and fulfillment can perceive this reality and stride forward to it.

The realization that you have built a shell around yourself is profound.

Once you acknowledge the state of being stuck, you can begin the journey of identifying and freeing yourself from this self-imposed confinement.

Many individuals remain unaware of this truth, believing their circumstances to be unbreakable walls. They fail to acknowledge it is just a shell they have constructed.

Understanding that you have woven this shell over the years means you also possess the power to shatter its constraints.

In fact, this is a monumental step toward freedom, fulfillment, and the exploration of untapped possibilities. Through this initial stride of awareness, you set out in the right direction, taking the first momentous step toward liberation.

Without the awareness of the shell that weighs heavily on you, your existence becomes one of pain and redundancy, void of fulfillment.

You will keep doing the same thing, and you will not be able to get out of it because you cannot grow beyond that shell.

The shell will never change in size. You are growing inside that shell, and eventually, it's going to feel very tight.

Being stuck in a shell is like living a repetitive life.

Each passing day becomes a haunting echo of the past. You're encountering the same problem over and over again. It's like Groundhog Day from the movie with Bill Murray, where he has to live the same day over and over again.

I don't know about you, but I would not like to live out my life in a tight shell.

Okay, so you don't either. Great.

So, you have to ask yourself questions. Engage in introspection and ask yourself fundamental questions such as the following:

How do you genuinely feel?

Are you authentically savoring the richness of life?

What impact have you made today? Did you celebrate significant victories?

On a scale of 1 to 5, how deeply satisfied are you with your life?

What would improve your life?

If you find yourself grappling with these questions and realize you have an unquenchable longing for a better life, yet struggle to make the necessary changes, then you're trapped.

Do you sense that life is meandering without purpose, repeating the same actions with predictable outcomes?

At this moment, you recognize your shell and feel the need to break free.

Do you long for fulfillment, a meaningful impact, and a purposeful existence?

If these questions resonate, then it's time you shatter the shell.

Unleash your capacity for a life of freedom, purpose, and fulfillment.

Your extraordinary gift has the power to transform not only your life, but also those around you.

It's time to break through.

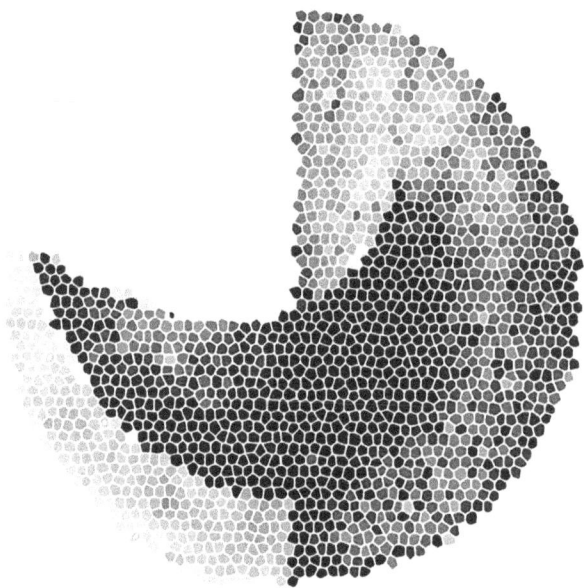

chapter two

Shock

Now that you understand that you are surrounded by some kind of shell, let me tell you what that shell represents.

It signifies all the false beliefs you have built in your life.

It's the script that you have in your subconscious that makes you act or react to things in a certain way.

When you are triggered and act a particular way, people react to how you act, and their reaction will reinforce your need to keep that shell.

But you don't realize it, right? You need to keep that protective barrier, your shell over your head.

This shell comes from somewhere, from that period in your life between the ages of 5 and 12. Our brains are like sponges and the line between subconscious and conscious is blurred.

During this period, our analytical mind is beginning to form, and we start to interpret meaning and draw conclusions about the laws of external life. Anything a child in this range is told, or any meaning they assign to an experience, will get planted into the subconscious without filter or logic.

So, the work we're going to do is identify this shell and from what situation in your childhood it came from.

Then we're going to work on how to break you free from it. However, the process will include shocking you because you're probably not expecting the origin, or how it's impacting you and those around you.

The shock is, "Oh my, I can't believe I've been doing the same things for so many years because of those negative patterns."

And naturally, it's hard for people because this shell is part of their identity.

The shock is when people are made to realize the meaning of their shell, where it's coming from, and the impact it has on their life. When they crack it open.

They say, "I didn't know I was doing this. Now I understand why people are like this. Now I know where this is coming from."

It makes sense that this is a shock.

But this shock is also what gives people the desire to actually try to get out of that shell.

They're shocked by the impact of their belief or pattern because now they understand what it's doing to them and where it's coming from.

So, let's talk about you.

What repetitive patterns or events happened to you between the ages of 5 and 12? How did your parents raise you? How did they interact with you? What traumatic event created this identity that you have built around you for many, many years?

Repeated over time, your response to these events turns into a pattern of behavior. We latch onto this behavior as a refuge, a safe place to go when we are triggered or upset. And it becomes our "go-to" behavior.

As a result, you keep doing things that make you feel like you're stuck.

Now, maybe you're in a situation where you're about to get divorced. Or maybe your career is falling apart.

You're about to lose everything you built because of that ugly and stinky mess you carried around.

Or it could be that you keep attracting the same type of people (as I did).

Well, you're reading this book for a reason, right?

You have a problem.

Your problem is that you're stuck in your life. You're lost. You feel like you keep repeating the same behavior.

So, you have a shell. You have an identity, a false identity that you have built over the years.

Now let's talk about how you need to recover.

It's very simple.

There are two choices: You can stay in your stinky mess and dwell in it, or we can find a way out.

The longer you stay in that mess, the more you're going to repeat your patterns.

For example, if you're going through a very bad divorce or other terrible situation, the more you hold on to it, refuse to change, and refuse to look at it, the more you're going to stay in that problem.

You definitely don't want that. And after all, you're reading this because you want to change.

You want to break free.

If you're ready for this, then let's go. I'm ready.

Before I take you through the process, I'm going to shock you with the impact that it has had on your life.

You're behaving in a way that makes people codependent on you.

You keep saying yes, and people become reliant on you as a result.

And when you don't deliver, what happens?

They complain.

For example, let's talk about your parents. Many men I work with are very respectful and don't want to hurt their parents.

Your parents didn't do this on purpose. They didn't know.

They did their best, but despite their best, you didn't receive any love. Maybe the only thing they wanted was for you to have A+ grades. So to get their attention, you needed to get that A+, but it was never enough.

Now, as an adult, you're going after people who have charisma and power over you. In return, you want your needs taken care of, but you don't get it.

You continue attracting people like your mom and dad.

This should be a shock for you.

The only way for you to get unstuck is to be shocked.

This shock is similar to an electroshock. It's like I'm shooting you with electricity and shaking you, saying, "You have to wake up!"

Without shock, you're going to be complicit.

You may do a little bit of work, but then you're going to go back to your comfort, that place that makes you feel at ease.

The shell is very tight, but it still feels safe.

Therefore, I'm going to have to shock you to make that fissure, and you're going to want to get out. I'm going to create an electroshock in you by unveiling the reality of the situation.

Right now, all you're feeling is a sensation. It's this feeling of being stuck.

However, I will show you the ugly and then the beauty because the only way you can desire a change is to be shocked by looking at the ugly.

If it's beautiful, what would you change? You'd say, "Oh, I like it. It's not that bad."

But if it's ugly, you'd say, "I can't. I have to get out of this. I'm done. I'm tired of pretending. I'm tired of dating the same people. I'm tired of doing the same thing. I have to change."

Once you see the ugly, we can start looking at what it would look like when it's beautiful and when you feel great.

How would it feel to be in that beautiful place?

You would feel free, loved, and like you're enough.

That's what you want.

I want you to take that desire and strength to push yourself out of this, so we can work on building that "muscle" together.

Now that you know it's ugly and stinky inside, and it's really beautiful outside, I need you to make it happen. I can create an opening for you, but I need you to push very hard.

Let's get out.

Let's do it together.

When you look at that ugly and stinky mess, you are now able to describe what is beautiful and what would be beautiful for you.

It's what you want to experience and what you're yearning for.

Now that you see the crap, your brain will automatically start to say, "I want to be able to experience something else instead. I don't want to see this anymore. I'm done."

It's the ugly and stinky mess that basically triggers the vision of beauty because you don't realize how bad it is until you see its impact on your life.

Its impact on you makes you now dream and imagine a world or a situation that is so much better for you. It's the one that you want. The one that you want to live in.

So let's get you out of this.

Now you can actually take advantage of the crack I created for you and get out of that shell.

Once you have that beautiful image, you have an incentive to make it happen.

You do that by making a commitment to say, "I am ready to work on myself. I am ready to change. I'm going to do it."

I don't want to see this ugliness anymore.

I'm ready. I want this beautiful life.

I've been living in this shell far too long.

I'm tired of living here.

I'm tired of being this person. I want to be happy again.

That's my motivation, and I'm going to get out of this shell.

I'm going to keep pushing. I'm going to keep doing my exercises.

I'm going to keep working on myself.

I'm going to keep noticing.

And every time I notice, it's going to give me a kick in the ass, an electroshock, because every time I look down, I'm going to get shocked as if I have a dog collar on.

I don't want to feel that pain anymore.

I want to look up.

I want to look up because I don't want to feel that shock every time I look down.

All my clients are ready to do the work because I have shocked them so hard that they don't want to stay in this ugly and stinky mess any longer.

Sometimes, some of them fail. They may fail for a month and say, "Oh, it's so hard." But even then they are making small improvements.

Eventually, they all change, because they start feeling better. The great feeling they get from the change is what makes them want to keep going.

If you're not open to the shock, you're wasting your time and money with me, or in this case, the price of the book.

Close the book. Why are you reading this? Send it back to the bookstore.

This is the process. I'm not a band-aid coach. This is how I work, and this is how the process works.

You want it? Great. I want you to embrace the shock and say, "This is a real thing. I need to accept it, and now I need to heal."

You must embrace it by seeing the reality and realizing it's painful. You need to acknowledge it and not fight it, so you can move in the right direction.

However, it's up to you. You can choose. At the end of the day, it's your choice.

You can choose to avoid it and stay where you are, or you can choose to embrace it and live a life of fulfillment.

It's up to you.

It isn't necessary for all the pressure to be resolved today. This process takes time and repetition.

If you fall down, it's okay. It's a journey. The pattern occurs subconsciously. We are usually totally unaware of it, and over time it starts to define us.

We tend to opt for safety. And since safety is one of our most basic needs, the primitive brain quickly chooses a behavior that allows us to feel safe again. Usually, safety is what we know, what feels comfortable.

The opposite of safety is the unknown. You can imagine that it's going to be great, but it's still unknown. When something is unknown, it feels uncomfortable, and the brain will naturally get defensive. That's just how we are. We're all like this. We all innately seek safety.

So, it's okay.

We'll just have to keep doing it and train the brain to understand that this is the new version we want to go towards.

Sometimes we'll fail, and that's okay. What's important is that we learn, and we try again.

Look at the Ugly

Look at the ugly, as I wrote about earlier. It's so important.

Go ahead. Do you feel alone? Do you feel that you're not enough, not important, and not loved?

Look at it.

Maybe you feel abandoned or not seen, and it's hard.

All you want is to shine, to do things that you enjoy, and to feel like you have room to grow. However, right now, you're not feeling that.

You feel like a mess. You may be doing drugs, watching porn, and destroying your body.

That's ugly.

You have lost everything as a result.

That's ugly.

You lost your family. You lost your home. You lost your job.

That's ugly.

Looking at the ugly is important because you have to acknowledge how bad it is and how much it is impacting your life.

The ugly is why you're reading this.

The ugly is what got you into the situation you are in today.

It's the same as if you were eating something and I told you it's bad for you. Unless I show you a picture of what it's doing to your body in real-time, you will keep eating it because it's really good.

If you want to face the ugly, then we need to go back in time and look at it from the beginning. Otherwise, it's hard to face and accept it if you don't understand where it all started.

You know it's real. You see it, but you have to understand where it's coming from. So, I'm going to help you connect the dots.

When we make that connection, you'll say, "Okay, I get it. Now I see what happened."

An example of the ugly would be if you married someone who is attractive, but is very cold and doesn't honor your needs. You've married a narcissist.

Another example would be if you've worked with people who literally take advantage of you, and there's no growth. They just want you to continue serving them and caring for their needs. You're never invited to any events or part of any groups, and you feel lonely.

All I'm doing is holding a mirror and showing you what you already know because when you're in the shell, you don't see anything.

All you know is that it doesn't feel right. So I have to mirror the ugly back.

You're not going to like what it looks like, and you need to understand where it's coming from. If you don't learn where it's coming from, you won't change. That's what's going to help.

Feel the Beauty

Now you might feel horrible and say, "I can't believe I made those choices. It was so hard to look at the ugly!"

However, at this point, at least you know what the ugly is, and where it's coming from.

Now I want you to imagine what it would feel like if this shell was no longer around you.

It might feel like love.

You might feel like you belong.

You might feel recognized.

You might feel safe.

You might love yourself.

You might feel stronger.

And when you face the beauty, you're going to feel amazing. It's like a little taste of sweetness.

You can taste the sweetness again after so many years of bitterness.

You feel like, "Oh, that's so good. I want more."

That's how it feels. It's that sense of sweetness, those endorphins, and a feeling of "I just want more. I'm excited about it. I'm super excited about it."

You will want more, and it just feels great.

And compared to what you feel right now?

It's heaven! You want to feel heaven.

You're done feeling like hell. You're done feeling the ugly.

How do you get there?

You get to the sweetness by imagining what a life without the shell will look like.

Imagine how you want this life to feel.

Now all the things you have been craving in life for so long are coming back to you. You begin dreaming again.

That's the taste of sweetness.

The feeling of joy will make you not want to go back to the shell again. Because it's so exciting, it's so inspiring, and it feels so good. You feel amazing, and you want more.

You're going to think, "Can I have more of that?"

You start to build that "muscle" of vision, and it's like a flow going into your brain.

It's going to get bigger and bigger, and you're just going to want more.

It's that feeling of freedom and joy. Everybody wants to experience that.

Push Hard

Pushing hard will bring you closer to the reality you're visualizing right now. Looking back will push it further away and make the journey longer and more painful.

Therefore, pushing hard is basically making sure you get a good part of your body out of the shell.

If you get a good push and can get both arms out of it, you'll have an easier time getting out because you have more strength.

The big push is the symbolic representation of the desire and the action and behavior you need to get out of your shell. Shifting your mind from the size and the feeling of the ugly, to imagining the beautiful life that you have access to, is what gives you that push.

It's that comparison and those feelings that give you extra strength because you prefer the sweetness over the bitterness.

Nothing will come to you if you don't work hard for it.

Nothing will come to you at all.

To work hard at this, you've got to focus your mind and your energy on the vision of that beauty.

So keep looking at that vision, that sweetness, feel like you're already there, and push.

I'm here by your side. I'm not leaving you.

I'm going to guide you through the process.

I'm not letting you down, but you've got to push with me. You've got to do it.

You have the strength, you have the muscle, you have the energy.

You've got this!

Look Down

Now it's time to look down.

Looking down is going back to where you were.

It's seeing where you came from. The same pattern of not going anywhere, feeling pain, and sometimes temporary joy.

Once you're shocked by looking at the ugly, and then you visualize and focus your energy on the beauty, the second time you look at the ugly, you're like, "I don't want this."

The more I stay in this ugly, the less I have access to this beauty that I'm yearning for.

So, I better move my ass.

Today is the day that I'm a new human.

Today is the day that I get out of this ugly mess.

Today is the day.

Looking down makes me vomit. It makes me feel disgusted. It makes me feel like this isn't me.

This is my old shell. I don't want this. I didn't sign up for this. I don't want this anymore. I'm done.

I'm ready to let go and heal. I'm ready to get out.

You will look down again, and you will truly know how it feels.

It's disgusting. It's sticky.

You can barely stand it anymore.

It's like sitting in your own piss.

You know the feeling when you're in the water, and you pee on yourself? It's warm, right?

Now imagine, you get out and clean yourself up, and someone says, "Now go back to your pee," it sounds disgusting. It protected you for a while because it was warm, but you don't want to return to this pool of urine. Not anymore.

I'm sorry. I know that analogy is a little disgusting, but I mean it. Think about it.

You're in the shell where there's no place to go, so you just relieve yourself in it. It feels warm, and it is a great feeling.

When you finally have the ability to get out, you see, "Oh, my bum is really red." And then, it feels really good when you put some cream on it.

Looking back at it, it's like, "I was sitting on this ugly mess for 20 years? Ugh. I'm not going back in it."

Don't go back.

Accept the Unknown

I'm finally me, the human I wanted to be.

I'm excited about the possibilities that I have in front of me. I'm excited about that woman or man, that amazing partner I'm going to meet.

I'm excited about feeling good, the amazing job or career I'm going to land, and all the things I'm going to be able to do.

I'm excited to have the life I've always dreamed about that I never knew I could have.

But now I know I can.

Hell yeah, I'm going to get it.

I'm not going back to the ugly.

Never again.

Accepting the unknown is to say, "I'm excited. I'm done. It feels great. That cream feels great. I'm not going back to that mess. I didn't even know I was sitting in my excrement that long. It's disgusting and it stinks. I can't believe I got used to the smell.

"I've been sitting on that mess for 20 years. Although it felt great at the time, it feels irritating now.

"So give me that healing ointment. I want that cream."

"I'm tired. I'm not going back to that mess. I'm not going back into that disgusting pool of waste."

Why would I?

It hurts and it was irritating.

Enough!"

Accepting the unknown is going to give you wings. It's going to provide you with the vision of what your gift is, what your potential is, and what you can do outside of that shell.

It's what you've missed out on by being in that shell.

It will show you how strong and amazing you are.

It's going to show you greatness, and you want to feel that greatness.

You will say, "I feel amazing!"

It's like the sweetness that tastes so good or the cream that relieves your rash. It's that feeling of being soothed and feeling amazing.

That's what it's going to do for you.

It's going to give you access to a world of possibilities you didn't know you had.

It's going to give you the ability to make a dent in the universe.

It's going to give you access to your gift.

It's going to give you wings to do the things you thought were impossible.

You didn't even know you had those gifts, but now you have them.

It's just amazing; it feels like you. It feels free. It feels extraordinary.

Without the shock, you'll be sitting in your mess for the rest of your life. I can tell you that it doesn't feel great.

It stinks, it hurts, and it's disgusting.

It's starving your needs.

It's missing opportunities, and it's being stuck. It's feeling pain.

You will age fast. Very fast.

It will make you sick.

If you want to look great and feel great, then you have to get yourself out of that disgusting mess you've been sitting in for so long.

There is a way.

It's doing things with joy and energy because energy boosts your immune system.

If you're happy, laughing, and having high energy, it's good for your body.

If you're depressed, anxious, and stressed, your immune system goes down and becomes weaker.

Therefore, it's going to help you feel great, and it's going to keep your health up.

You're going to want to eat better because you're going to say, "I want to look amazing.

"I'm going to eat healthy. I want to start working out.

"I'm just going to look sharp.

"I'm going to stand up straight.

"I'm going to look different.

"I'm going to be attractive. Attractive in every sense. I can attract the right job. I can attract the right people. I can attract the right opportunity because I'm standing up straight.

"I'm attractive. I'm no longer hunching over, sitting in my mess, and living a flatlined life.

"Now I have a pulse. I have high energy that will keep me energized and looking amazing. I feel good."

Who doesn't want to feel the rush of those endorphins?

Who doesn't want to feel good?

You need to be shocked because no one wants to stay in their ugly and stinky mess for that long.

Do you want to live a life of possibility?

Do you want to live a life of purpose?

Do you want to start smelling the roses?

Do you want to feel amazing?

If you answered "yes," then take my hand. Let's get out of that shell.

I promise you that when you come out of your shell and start looking forward to the life you've always wanted, you will never be sitting in that stinky mess again.

That stuff is going to be gone for good.

But if you don't go through the shock, you will continue sitting in it.

You now recognize that your life was disgusting. You didn't know you were sitting in that repulsing mess, but now you do, and your action is to push ahead. Break out.

Remind yourself that you were sitting on it for far too long. Your bum hurt. It stunk. You didn't feel great. You felt pain. You didn't feel growth. You didn't feel recognized. You didn't feel anything. You were numb.

That stinky mess can be gone.

It's going to be gone. It's going to be far, far away.

Do you see the opportunity?

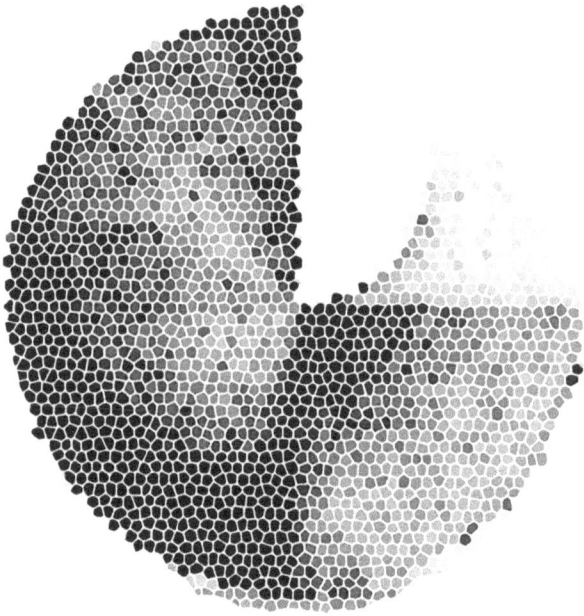

chapter three

Seed of Awareness

The seed of awareness comes after we realize that we have a shell, and we've found the area where we can crack it.

That's when you recognize that you can get out of it. You become aware, and that is so important.

I may end up shocking you (as in the last chapter), but I want to ask you again, "Do you want to stay here? Do you want to stay in this ugly and stinky mess you've been in for 30 years? Or rather, do you want to see what's outside of your shell? Do you want to see what's waiting for you, and what's available, what opportunities you have?"

I hope by now you will say, "Yes, I want to get out of this."

After that conversation with my clients, I work to plant a seed, where I basically share what the limiting or false beliefs are, causing all of this. This is where you start to become more aware of them and where they're coming from. That's the point of the seed of awareness.

So, let's start by understanding why you created all these layers. What made you realize that you were stuck in this shell? It's all the things you built over the years, and all the experiences that have happened to you, and the situations you've attracted.

Now you have to realize that these things are subconsciously created, making them real is what kept you in that shell.

You can now see that there's a problem, and you know what this problem is, so let's build on this.

I need to bring you back to where it all began: it started between the ages of five and twelve. So what happened during that time that made you believe this?

It could be situations like this: "My dad was very hard on me. No matter what I did, it didn't matter. It was never enough. I would bring home an A-plus, but it wasn't enough."

It could be, "I was fat, I was different, and I was never getting invited anywhere," or, "My mom was very abusive," or "I never felt warmth or love from my parents."

Now you can see that, because of that absence you had, you believe that's your reality, so you built a shell around it. You were accepting it as reality and as truth.

However, what evidence do you have that those things are true?

What is true is that you believed it, but what's

not true is what you believe because of it, or what you believe you are as a result of it.

We need to change that belief, but before we can do that, you have to be aware of where it's coming from and how it affects your life today.

If you understand that you're not feeling loved, what happens? Do you seek love, demand it, and become very needy? What happens when you don't get it? Do you seek it from somewhere else?

Do you work your ass off and say "yes" to too many things? Do you feel like a "jack of all trades?" Do you do whatever people want and feel like it's never enough, and now you're exhausted?

Do you now see the correlation between what you experienced during that early stage of life and the result of it today? That's the seed of awareness.

Now, what do you want to do with that?

Obviously, this person you are now seeing is not who you really are. The behavior patterns do not define you. So let's change things.

This is not your own self. You only adopted it.

You thought that's how life should be, but the reality is different.

Let's change this, and work on replacing this mindset with something better, such as the feeling that you are enough, and that you are loved.

Now, you're aware.

We've identified the problem, where it's coming from, and identified the pain and what it does to you today.

You're aware of the consequences, or the feeling you have today, so now we can work on changing things.

Congratulations, you have the seed of awareness.

Now that you are aware of what has been keeping you inside your shell and you are shocked at the impact that it has had on your life, you can connect the dots with the origin and where it all started.

You can put the pieces together and realize you've been adopting it. It's not yours.

Now you start to work on figuring out how to you override it and rewrite your story.

How can you replace this belief? This belief of thinking that you're not enough, not loved, a failure, not important, not safe, or whatever.

How do you change your behavior patterns?

You've got to change, and believe you can change.

It starts with accepting that you're not that person anymore. Then you will create a new identity that is the one that you want.

But to do this, you will need to completely get out of your former shell, and be ready to go onto the path you're destined to take.

Then you can grab that gift and that space in the universe that was destined for you.

Start at the Beginning

I start by asking who you are today and the problems this is causing you. When we need to identify that, we'll go back to asking what you believe in.

You might say, "Well, I believe that I'm not loved."

When did this happen? When did this situation that you're in start? What comes to mind?

If you think, "I'm not loved. I'm not heard. I'm not enough," this is where I'm going to explain to you what it means in reality.

Again, now is the time to connect the dots with what you have experienced between the ages of five and twelve.

For example, if you say, "I feel like I'm not enough," usually there are three most common reasons you have decided this.

One, your parents' love for you was conditional on you meeting their high expectations. And they used shame and criticism when you failed to meet them.

Two, one of both parents were models of standards that were either too high or were misaligned.

Lastly, your feeling of not being enough could have been the direct correlation of your compensating for feeling deprived, socially excluded, or like a failure.

That basically makes you feel and believe that you're not enough as you grow into an adult, right? Because you believe that that's what life is.

It's the same thing with love. If you always say, "I want a hug, I want your attention," and your parents say, "No, we don't have time," that's what love is for you because you didn't see it shown by your parents.

You always asked, "Can I have a hug? Can I have love? If I do this, can I have that?" Then, as an adult, you have noticed that you're trying to do things for people in order to get love. But who do you ask? You ask people who do not give you love. Cold and charismatic people.

To make a long story short, you keep getting the same results because you continue acting the same way and attracting the same people. So it's just reinforcing the belief that you need to stay in that stinky mess.

"That's just what life is. This is my identity. I guess I'm not enough, I'm not loved, and I'm not needed.

"I'm alone. That's the reality, I suppose.

"Not only that, but I'm still miserable. I don't feel right.

"Maybe I need help because I don't know how to get out of it.

"I don't know what to do, and I'm stuck here."

Go back to the beginning, and start looking at the patterns that showed up in your life.

Patterns of Fake Reality

You've got to look at patterns.

Between the ages of five and twelve, your beliefs are formed and solidified, and they become permanent in your mind.

Each belief has been continuously patterned, and it emerges again and again, to a point where it becomes normal for you.

For example, you might consistently have a pattern that says, "No, it's not enough. Go back. You can do better."

Or it could start with, "Mom, I would love to confide in you. Can I share with you?" And she says, "No, I don't need to hear this."

It's the same behaviors that are repetitive, and once they are cemented in, you will keep seeing them throughout your life.

Good beliefs that cement in place during this time are love and ideal relationships. But it runs the gamut. Perhaps you believe that if you just keep working, you can actually achieve that amazing state of perfection. You just have to keep working hard, and imagine an end to the road. The point where you can finally relax and enjoy life. That's what it is. That's all you know. It may not make you happy, but it is familiar. It is the devil you know.

The challenge is that peace never comes. Even if it did, you would just find something else to do. This is how your belief reinforces itself. What you are observing today is the outcome of that.

If your belief became "work harder", now you see those people who say, "You want more work? Okay. Here you go."

Because now you attract those people who are going to feed and validate that belief, and they're going to keep reinforcing it.

A perfect example, and the most common one I see, is, "I'm not enough."

Why? Because many parents have high expectations or are models of high and misaligned standards.

So what happens? Now you focus on achievement and therefore react in a certain way with people, like a boss who asks, "Hey, can you do this?"

You say, "Oh, sure, I'll do it. Okay, I'll do it. I can totally do it. Give it to me."

And you'll do it because your reward is a measure of success and you expect something in return. You'll think, "I will get praise. I'm going to prove I'm enough."

But what happens is that you become overwhelmed because you take on too much. Your health might be suffering because of the daily over-work stress. Too much energy goes into keeping your life in order or feels like constant pressure while working without any fun.

After a while, the feeling of being overwhelmed makes you think, "I am physically exhausted. I don't have any fun. I am not happy. My marriage is suffering. My health is suffering. I don't have any time for myself. Something is wrong."

Now people feel frustrated, irritated, and disappointed in you when you take on more than you can realistically deliver on and then let them down.

They are yelling at you and saying, "What are you doing? You told us that you would do this."

In your head, you're thinking, "Others don't value me. I'm never enough. They always want more from me than I can realistically give. They expect more from me than they do from others. I do the work for everybody, and every time I get the same thing. It's never enough."

Go back to your childhood. Who said that?

Your dad? Your mom?

Once my clients realize the source of the problem, they usually think, "I think it's that I always see the light at the end of the tunnel. I think that when I get there I can relax and have what I want. I feel like I am getting there."

Or they may say, "Oh my God. Now I see. That's exactly what I experienced."

"I've got to stop this. I can't do this anymore."

"How am I going to change this?"

"It's so hard."

Well, the effect these patterns have on your life today is that you are suffering. That's why you're reading this. You're exhausted, and feel as though you don't get anything in return no matter what you do.

It's never enough. You've tried everything.

You try to keep adding more work, but it's still not working.

You've tried a therapist, but it did not help.

You're consumed, and you're at a point where your health is failing. Your work-life balance feels unbalanced. Your relationships are negatively impacted.

You're not doing the work you're supposed to be doing. You procrastinate a lot, because your belief makes many tasks feel overwhelming, so you avoid them.

Your voice is saying, "I cannot keep up with the

load of work. I can't satisfy people anymore. I can't make them happy.

"I'm not happy. My needs are not met.

"I'm depleted, I'm empty, I have nothing left.

"I need help. I just don't know what to do."

So let's connect the dots.

Look back to the ugly mess.

Look back to the beliefs you don't want hanging around your neck.

If you know where it's from, and you know it's not you, that it's just the circumstances that have created that belief and are now causing the problem, you will no longer own it.

You can say, "This is not mine. I want to be me."

Let's dive a little deeper. Let's say that you are raised by parents that aren't very loving, or affectionate, or don't give you enough time and attention, or maybe never provide you with a sense of direction.

They're just parents, right? They feed you, maybe pay for your school, and whatever you need, but they just don't express any love to you or give you any attention.

It's natural to want to try to get their attention because we're born with that need for love.

You're going to do things to grab their attention, hoping that you will receive it. You become demanding.

That pattern is what you will carry with you as an adult as you grow up with a core grief over the absence of a nurturing parent.

Who do you attract in your life now?

Chances are that the people you attract are emotionally unavailable people, super charismatic and cold.

As a result, you become disappointed or even angry and demanding if your needs are not met. You may constantly blame others of not caring enough about you. Even if you attract the appropriate partner who is emotionally giving, you can sabotage the relationship by becoming distant and unreachable.

Does that sound familiar?

You attract the same identity because of what you experienced as a child.

Your pattern is being with people who are hard to receive love from.

When it comes to beliefs, It doesn't matter if it's your biological mom and dad. It could be people that you've been close to during that time. It could be a teacher, a friend, or maybe a family friend, but as long as those patterns keep happening, that's what's going to affect you.

But of course, the people that you see the most are the ones that have the most influence on you. The people you see from time to time might have an impact, but it's going to be very mild, unless you experienced a traumatic event.

In fact, this could be about any trauma that may have happened. For example, if a child loses a parent or sees a parent disappearing from their lives between the ages of five and twelve, they may develop the abandonment belief because it's something that has impacted them.

You Didn't Ask for it

It's important to separate yourself from the pattern because you didn't ask for those consequences.

You were born with love.

You came into this life completely naked, with love, and then you got a life you didn't ask for.

Your childhood's life just came to you.

You didn't ask to grow up in a family where there was no love pattern.

You have to be aware of that, so you can understand why you don't want it.

This is where it's very hard for people because of course they love their parents.

I'm not asking you not to love your parents, or to hate them. I'm asking you to forgive them instead. Forgiveness is the best tool and the best way to actually detach from those consequences.

After all, your parents didn't know. They were most likely also raised with a lack of love or with high standards for example, which is all they knew. They just repeated what they had learned, so you can't completely blame them.

You can't say, "This is your fault. This is all because of you." You must forgive.

If you don't forgive, you can't move on.

Forgiveness is so critical, and it's a key step in detaching from these things that are not yours.

Then what?

You're free.

Now you're free to start moving forward.

You've freed yourself from this weight that has been on you, that you've been carrying all your life.

It's like you've been putting all these beliefs in your bag, and you just carry it around over the years. It's getting heavier and heavier, but now you're giving yourself permission to let go.

You don't need to carry it.

What is in the bag is not yours. You've got to let go of it. When you let go, you forgive.

It's like you're getting rid of all these weights and in the context of the shell, it's what kept you down. It's what kept you inside that shell and made it feel tight. Now it's like you're letting go and loosening it up. You're losing those ties, so now you can get out of it. That's what it does to you, it frees you.

I'm not asking you to forget.

I'm not asking you not to love anymore.

What I'm asking you to do is to accept that it wasn't intentional. When people do that to their children, it's because that's all they know.

Even in my story with my abusive mom, I have

forgiven her for her actions. That's why I have no resentment, because that was what kept me inside my shell. It was that tether.

You don't want that. You want to forgive. You still want to love your parents for what they thought was best.

You just want to freely get out of it, and to be able to live the life you were meant to live, not the one that you thought you should live.

The one that you choose.

Adopted Reality vs. Created Reality

Adopted reality is something that you took on from others, and you made it yours, subconsciously thinking that's what it should be.

If it's their reality, then it's going to be mine, of course! I'm their son, or their daughter, or their student, or their friend, or whatever.

Since it's a pattern, you think it's a reality, so the adopted reality is what you take on as yours.

The created reality is your true reality, without that adopted weight that has been holding you down.

Your adopted reality reinforces the patterns you experienced as a child. They reinforced that false truth, that false reality. They fortified that adopted reality. They said, "You're not enough," so you thought, "I guess I'm still not enough. This is just reality."

The created reality is the one you chose. It's the one you wanted and created as a result of setting yourself free.

It's what you create when you let go of resentment or anything that is pulling you back into that shell and into that space you no longer desire.

The created reality is the one I like. It's the one I chose, that sets me free.

I get to be in my power seat, meaning that I no longer have that feeling of being stuck.

I'm no longer holding that false identity with me,

and I'm more in alignment with who I believe I am.

In this newly created reality, people are transformed. They are no longer the people who are taken advantage of because they feel they are not enough.

They are the people who get hugged and loved.

They are the people that get invited to events, get included, and feel they belong.

They are the people that make you feel safe, and they are the people you surround yourself with that make you feel right.

You feel free.

You feel more like yourself, and you don't have to go back into that shell again.

It's simple. If you feel like you're still struggling and are still seeing some pattern or the behaviors of certain people in yourself, there are still some things to let go of.

As you're creating this new reality that you desire, as you forgive people, as you're letting go of resentment, and whatever is weighing you down, you're stripping yourself out of this false identity, your shell.

There will be some people who will want to bring you back in because they liked your old self and you were serving them. It may be that they don't like the new person you're becoming.

That's when you know that you have to let go of these people. It's time. And that's okay!

These people are no longer the people you need to surround yourself with because these people like the old you. They still have their own shell, so they want to bring you into that shell because it worked perfectly for them.

If they don't want to accept you and join you on this journey, then you know you've got to let go of them.

Think about it. You're trying to get out of your shell, and they are trying to push you back in, saying, "Just stay in that shell! We don't want you to get out!"

If they see who you're becoming, and you're transforming, and they say, "Oh, we like that. We want to get out too, we want to do the same," then you're inspiring them.

These are the people who will follow you. They want to be inspired and motivated to actually get out of their own shell. They're changing, too, and they're no longer the ones that want to keep you there.

Anything that is trying to bring you back to your old self is what you want to get rid of, and it's going to take time.

Change doesn't happen overnight. As everyone knows, it's a journey in which we never stop growing.

However, as long as you don't look back and keep moving forward, you'll get stronger and stronger.

All these things weighing on you will shed slowly and be replaced by something stronger, something you love, something that makes you happy.

Eventually, these people that were trying to pull you back will be gone.

All the situations that were pulling you back will all gone.

They will have disappeared.

New Behaviors = New Beliefs

You feel different.

You've come a long way since the first time we met.

You're no longer that person who came to me and said, "Nora, I don't feel right. I'm stuck. I don't know where I am going."

You don't feel that anymore. You feel different, like you have more space.

You see the people around you changing, and you like that. You have a different experience.

You feel empowered in your new truth.

You feel stronger and things are changing.

For example, you're now starting to go up the ladder. You're growing in your career.

You find the love of your life, that person who is going to truly love you. You finally find that woman or that man who makes you feel good about yourself and brings the best out of you.

You now have the desire to go to the gym. You're joining groups, you feel different, you feel happy, you feel empowered, you feel strong, and you feel confident.

If I were to make a comparison of how you were when you came to me and now, you'd say, "Uh, that was me?"

You like what you've become, and you like where you're going.

Here's another way to look at it. When someone looks down and says, "Oh, I'm miserable," I say, "What do you see?"

They say, "Well, I see my shoes. I see the floor."

I ask, "What does it look like?"

They are not impressed, so I say, "Okay, let's lift your head. What do you see?"

They say, "I can see the sky, the horizon!"

That's the effect. When you look at the floor, it's brown. But when you look up, it gets lighter and lighter, and then it's blue. Blue is a nice color to see. In fact, blue is the color of purpose.

If you notice the change, it's quite significant.

It is the change from looking down at your stinky mess to looking up at the blue sky of your possibility.

"I didn't know the sky was so blue. I've been looking at the floor for 30 years."

It's like when you run. If I say, "Okay, go for a run," you'll say, "I don't want to run."

I'm pretty sure you're going to feel amazing if you do go running. But, okay, let's just walk for a little bit.

Then let's do a little jog. Now let's accelerate.

By the time we're done running, you feel amazing. You feel like a million bucks.

Why? Because you have a bunch of endorphins in your brain that make you feel like a Christmas tree. You say, "I feel amazing."

That's when I'd say, "I told you that!"

You were sitting, looking at the floor, and I was telling you, "Lift your head! Let's go for a run! You'll feel different!"

You'll realize, "Why didn't I do that for so many years?"

Now you know.

That's the feeling. It's a feeling of being more in tune with yourself.

Now you realize that you were in a shell that was not yours. It was an identity that was false that you thought was true.

You thought that's how life should be because you observed those patterns pretty much all your life, yet there was something wrong.

You knew you didn't feel right. You didn't know what it meant, but you needed help.

Now I'm showing you that this feeling is not yours.

Good work on this!

Now you can feel free.

You don't have any anger or anything that is holding you back.

You don't have any negative feelings, negative thoughts, or a negative mindset that keep you inside anymore.

You feel amazing.

If you're wanting to wallow in your stinky mess for another 30 years and complain about it, that's your problem.

And what's more, I say, if you're going to stay in it for another 30 years, you can't complain about it.

But if you decide it's time for change because it is not yours anymore, and you don't want this crap in your life, then let's go!

If you don't make that change, you're going to be in that mess until you die. And guess what? Not only are you going to be that stinky until you die, but you're going to carry so many regrets with you.

Regrets of not having a sense of accomplishment, or living a legacy.

You're not going to feel like you've made a difference.

You're just going to die lonely in your freaking crap with an ugly feeling.

And if you have children, now they're going to inherit your ugly mess.

Is that what you want to do to yourself and the people you love?

If you love them, you'll want to change.

If you want to get out and don't want that reality, and you want an alternative reality, then you've got to be aware of what's going on. You need to know where it's coming from, along with those patterns that have been planted in your subconscious and are now causing you to feel gross and stuck.

It's time to make a difference, and it is time to change.

You want to get rid of that weight, get rid of that resentment, get rid of that negative pattern, and be the person you were meant to be.

You can make a difference. You can access those opportunities that were meant for you.

Otherwise, you will stay in your stinky mess, die in it, and leave it behind as your legacy.

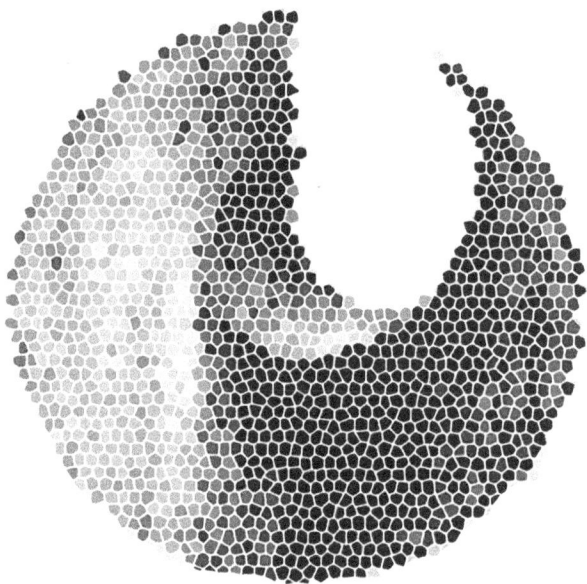

chapter four

Superpower

Your superpower is the talent you were born with. It's the gift that helps you make a dent in the universe.

These are the things that you are good at, and you become so passionate about that you can do them for hours on end. They make you feel happy, fulfilled, and even energized.

We were all born with them, but some of us don't pay attention to them because we live our lives on autopilot. And sometimes, we do it so naturally that we don't even realize we're using them, and some of us only utilize a part of them.

So, what should we do? We need to name, understand, focus on, and develop our superpowers, to reach our highest potential.

When I work with my clients to figure out their superpowers, I ask them to give me a list of things that people say about them.

What are the things that people thank you for?

What's something that you do every day that comes naturally to you?

What's a list of activities that you do pretty much on a daily basis? Are they energizing or draining?

Now, go back in time.

What was something that you did when you were a child, and that you would do for hours?

When you look at everything you do, focus on what is energizing you.

That's how we get started.

Then we try to find keywords of the things that come to mind when you think about your superpowers because we want to name them and talk about them. Identifying them gives us a chance to explain them to other people.

I usually tell people to do that with a résumé. I don't mean that the traditional way. I just want you to write about what you're gifted with, and what your superpowers are about.

When I do this exercise with people, their résumé is filled with all the things they enjoy, the things that energize them, and what they're good at.

That's one way to identify and "see" your superpowers. Another way to find them is to be aware of the activities you do.

Feel the energy while doing them because it's draining to do things not within your superpowers. What's more, if you keep doing them, it won't make a positive impact in your life or in this world. Eventually, they will become a heavier

Nora Paxton

and heavier load on you, because you're not getting fulfillment from them.

If you don't tap into your superpowers, and if instead, you only do things that aren't exciting, you'll live a flat and draining life.

But when you find things that you absolutely love, it will make a difference in terms of emotion, energy, and drive.

It's like the saying, "Do what you love, and you'll never work a day in your life."

You'll do things with a bigger impact, and create a bigger ripple effect.

Your superpower is the fuel that is going to help you make the changes you were meant to make, and the results will be incredible.

Find that superpower.

And when you tap into your superpower, just go at the speed of light.

You Have a Superpower

Imagine you're a superhero with a superpower, and your superpower is to move buildings or travel from one place to another in a second.

How would it feel?

You don't even have to go through the airport and check in. In one second, you're in a different place.

That saves you time. You can get to places much more efficiently, and you don't have to wait because you can move faster.

That's what superpowers do.

They accelerate the momentum that you're building. They accelerate the impact you want to make in this world.

The thing about video games, where most of us "think" we have superpowers, is that they only give you instant energy, not real superpowers.

For a moment, video games can give you a high dose of cortisol that can keep your brain very active. But as soon as it stops, you shut down.

That's why kids are bored and don't know what to do, because they spend their time playing video games. There's no other thing to keep them busy.

Instead, look up from your game of Candy Crush or whatever it is you're doing, and think about the "real" superpowers all around you.

An example of a superpower is the ability to see patterns and build solutions from them. Imagine an accountant who has been crunching numbers and building models for a long time.

Good data analysts, for example, can anticipate what would come next in the pattern of numbers and data. Because they are so good at it, they can build those models much faster than someone who has just learned it as a skill. It comes more naturally to them. Since it comes naturally to them, it's not an extra effort.

Imagine how much time you could save in a company if you were to have that gift, that superpower.

You could anticipate risks at a much faster speed, but you would also be excited because you would be saving the company and your clients from potential problems. All because this is your gift, and you are good at it.

Another good example is an opera singer. A person who has this amazing gift of having a stunning voice.

You're just a little girl or little boy, and you sing. You do a regular job, but you've developed this gift and realize that you get so much energy while singing. You realize that people around you enjoy your voice, and it makes them happy.

You say, "That's what I want to do. I want to sing! That's what gives me energy."

So you go to a singing school, and it comes easy to you. You already know you're gifted with this, so the practice is energizing.

The energy you're getting through singing and making people around you happy just by hearing your voice is a superpower.

A superpower is energizing, because you still feel its impact even after you're done using that power.

You're looking forward to the next time, and you keep that high because you're excited about the result of your energies. This is because you were born with a talent and are passionate enough to continuously develop it.

Sadly, there are some people who don't develop their talents. They know such powers are in them, but they choose a different path.

However, your talents are in you and will always be calling you.

It's time to start listening for them, and engaging them!

Energy Trail

When we're kids, we naturally gravitate towards our superpower.

Go back in time and remember what you did for hours as a child, and see if that activity would still be energizing today.

If nothing feels energizing, then that's where we need to have a deeper talk about the shell, the thing that's getting in the way of you seeing what's energizing.

We've got to remove whatever is clogging your feelings.

We cannot identify your superpower if we don't remove what's blocking your mind.

In fact, I usually don't start my clients with their superpowers right away. First, I remove anything that might hinder them from sharing what they really want and are good at. That's why I have them go back in time.

Let's do that for a moment.

When was the last time you were happy?

Do you remember that time when you felt that way?

What were you doing?

What was something that energized you?

Can you describe that scene?

I bring them back to that moment to figure out what made them happy.

Let's follow that energy trail where it leads.

Now think about your superpowers again. What energized you as a child?

How did you feel?

Hi, My Name is...

Identifying your superpower is an essential step. Let's try it, actually. We can use words like, "I'm a learner," or "I'm an architect," or you can say, "I build."

Craft a sentence that says, "My superpower is ... that I can sort through the chaos and turn it into something meaningful."

It could be, "My superpower is passion," or "My superpower is joy."

A superpower could be, "I'm very strategic."

A superpower could be, "I'm an idea person. I love ideas. I'm very good at generating ideas."

A superpower could be, "I'm a connector. I'm

very good at connecting people or connecting things."

You could say, "I'm a chef. I make food. I create food that delights the palates. That's my super-power. I delight palates."

Or "I'm an artist."

It comes easily once you identify what it is.

So if you just put a sentence or a word on it, what would be that word?

What would be the name that you want to give it?

You need to be able to describe it. When you give it a name, it feels like it's yours. It's your name, and it becomes part of your identity.

It's something that you can call out, and it's something that you can explain with pride.

It's who you are as a whole.

I have learned from experience that you feel like you understand it more when you name it. You can explain it, and you can express it.

When you give it a name, it will become clear to you.

You will own it.

Describe it

Next, how will your superpower help the world or other people?

For example, let's say the name I have given my superpower is, "I'm a personality expert."

Okay, great. So what do you do?

"I help people see their inner beauty and power, so they can use them to make a difference in their lives and the lives of others."

Fantastic.

If you are a chef, what makes it a superpower to you when you cook?

For example, let's say that when you cook, you feel like time slows down and you're traveling the world. You delight people's palates, and it makes them happy.

That gives you so much joy because you see that what you are creating is giving people happiness. They have had a bad day, but they come in, they sit down at your table, they eat the food you cooked, and now they are feeling delighted.

They leave that space with a lot of joy and energy because they had a great meal that really made them travel. You have people who keep coming back over and over because of the great food you cook. They're talking about your food all over the world.

As for you, you're enjoying it because you can keep doing it.

You could describe it as, "I create food that delights the palates of others."

Think about your superpower as something you're doing exceptionally well and consistently.

And describe it that way!

Focus and Fuel

You know where you're going now. You know your focus. And you've got your superpower.

You're motivated because you get positive results, positive feelings, and positive energy.

You can fuel your superpower by practicing it regularly, and using it every day.

I use my superpower all the time. I do coaching with people every day, and I get fueled by this work.

I use it on a daily basis. I live with it and do it as a business. I see the results of it in my clients as I experience their transformation with them and as I see them share their experience with others.

I get energized by that.

But, there can be too much of a good thing.

I make sure that I have a balanced life, so I can be more refreshed and have more clarity and energy.

I practice self-care to make sure I take care of myself.

You need to take care of the body that is carrying that superpower, so you can make it last longer. You can't just keep using it to the extreme.

Overusing your superpowers becomes a weakness and can become draining.

You want to keep that gift alive.

If you don't get enough sleep or eat well, you'll eventually deplete.

Therefore, make sure you take care of yourself and don't get carried away in the process of using your superpower.

For example, let's say you're so passionate about drawing that you're working on it too much. You spend hours doing it, but don't move from your chair.

Eventually, you're going to have problems with your back, hand, or wrist.

You're going to develop health issues that hinder you from using those superpowers because you overused them.

Imagine the excitement and energy you get by doing something you are exceptionally good at and love every day.

Compare that feeling to sitting at a boring job you're not excited about, but you do it because you can tolerate it.

Something in you is missing. You're not tapping into the power that you've been given at birth. You're not tapping into that flame that is within you.

We've all been given a gift, and you have the opportunity to develop it, make it a part of you, and make it the fuel of your life.

When you do that, you wake up every day with purpose.

You are excited about your day, the impact you're going to have, and the feeling you're going to get.

There's more out there for you.

This is your legacy to this world. This is the print that you leave behind.

You were meant to put your piece in this puzzle.

Imagine the power of your piece in this world when you complete that scene. It finally looks finished. It looks beautiful. It looks impactful.

That's what you need to figure out. That's what you need to tap into.

This is not something where you're sitting at a freaking desk or doing a job that's not fulfilling.

You have a mission. You have a calling. You have a purpose on this planet.

Find your superpower and take care of it. Make it stronger.

In the end, what we're going to remember is what you left to this world.

How you changed people's lives.

How you made a difference.

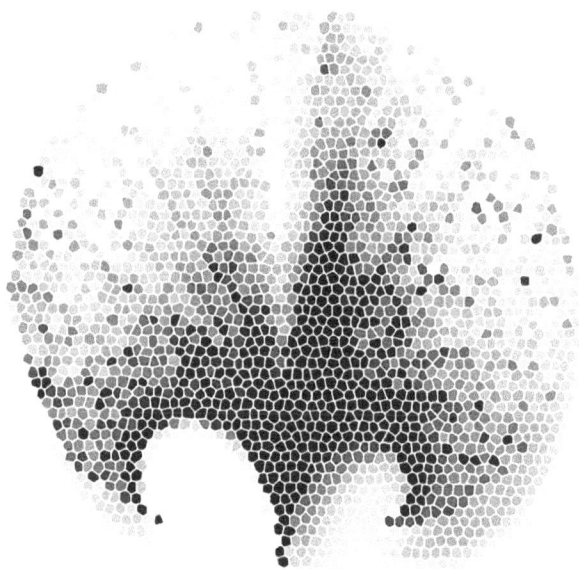

chapter five

Safety

It's time to grow and spread your wings. Feel the sunshine. Bask in that freedom.

As you use the gifts you have, feel that sense of accomplishment, beauty, love, and success.

That's when the concept of safety comes into play.

But the only way to attain a feeling of safety and security is to let go of whatever is holding you back.

This is especially relevant for people who come from a culture where there is a lot of inherent respect for one's parents. As I spoke about in earlier chapters, many of us feel we owe our parents a debt of gratitude. We respect how we were raised and recognize all the sacrifices they made for us, even if we were raised with tough love, or even abuse.

Some people never connect their problems to their childhood or their parents. They think, "It's me. I have a problem," or "It's my boss." Or they just assume that this is what life is all about.

However, when you connect the dots for them, and they realize, "That's my dad," or "That's my mom. Now I see the impact," it's hard for them. They have so much respect for their parents and don't want to hurt them.

I am writing about this again, because it's important to harp on certain things.

Now my clients often begin to see that something is wrong. They realize there's a relationship between their parents and the shell they've created for themselves.

They want to get out, but they feel like they're betraying the people who raised and cared for them.

Essentially, the work I'm doing is liberating them from those beliefs. I'm freeing them from that cocoon they've put themselves in, so they can fly, but safely.

They feel safe to be themselves and safe to use their gifts, without hurting their parents.

We're not here to call your parents and say, "You screwed me!" We don't say that.

The work we're doing is to find that sense of safety so that you can feel like you're good now. You're letting go of those beliefs and the hurt you got from your parents.

You're safe to go now, and you don't have to feel attached to that anymore.

When I say "safety", that could be misinterpreted as meaning "comfort zone". But don't get me wrong.

Comfort doesn't necessarily mean something is good for you, even if that's all you've ever known. You'll eventually outgrow it.

Comfort doesn't let you see what you're missing and what's out there. It doesn't let you see the opportunities in front of you that could completely transform your life, that could completely change your outlook.

However, the important thing is eventually realizing that comfort is actually not good for you and keeps hurting you.

You're this little caterpillar. You put all these layers on and cover yourself with this shell.

Then you have to shed.

It must be very painful to shed, have that whole transformation, and eventually fly away.

But now you're lighter, and you don't have all this ugliness.

You're actually beautiful.

The transition is painful, but it made you stronger.

I'm here throughout the whole process, so we're going to get through it safely. Through the discovery, the acknowledgment, the realization, and the forgiveness.

I'll hold your hand virtually and say, "You're good. I'm here, and everything is going to be okay."

That pain is the message that we are going to carry to share with the people who need to hear it so you can help someone else.

You need to realize that you are safe.

You just have to believe it.

The other side is safe. It's actually better.

Not a "comfort zone", but a "safe" one.

Connect the Dots

As I am always saying, you need to connect the dots by looking at patterns.

Based on the pattern, you identify the possible causes that could have led to those patterns and the situation you are in.

What are the patterns?

What things are you doing over and over again?

What are the common triggers?

What are the things that put you in this situation?

Then we analyze those patterns. I say, "Well, does that sound familiar to you? Does that remind you of something?"

At this moment, we connect it to the past as we're trying to figure out what this reminded you of.

You will never be set free if you don't recognize these patterns. You will always be in the same situation. It's only a matter of time. You will still be attracting the same people. You will still be addicted to whatever it is you're doing.

And you know what happens when you're addicted. If you have those patterns, it can lead you down the wrong path or lead to death, sickness, and loneliness.

The longer you retain this harmful pattern, the greater the risk to your life, and the harder it's going to be for you to get out of this.

It can get lonely. And when it does, you keep yourself stuck in that shell and never get out of it.

You're solidifying your pattern, and basically giving up.

You shouldn't do that.

Band-aid solutions won't help either because they are only temporary reliefs. They are not actually freeing you. You are still connected to your shell.

This is why you have to connect the dots, so you know why it's happening and understand it. Then you can forgive, let go, and experience that transformation.

Otherwise, there is no way you can go through that process. You will always come back to the same pattern.

I have given a few examples in the book so far of how parents can help to create beliefs within us, but there are many more.

You may have had loving parents who let you do anything you wanted. But as a result, you never had a structure.

Now you end up making a ton of mistakes because you wish you had some lessons and structure.

Or maybe your parents are loving, but they struggle financially. The financial struggle makes you develop a feeling of, "I'm not enough. It's never enough."

For this reason, you say yes to everything because you're afraid of scarcity. And you work too much because you are scared of being poor.

This doesn't mean that you don't have love. You attract very loving people into your life and work, but your sense of scarcity takes over those relationships.

These types of people become very successful. They actually do well, but they end up sacrificing their time. They stop giving time to themselves and the people they love.

There are so many cases that we could go through.

Maybe you were not loved, but you had a lot of money. Maybe you were overweight and got bullied when you were young. It comes in different ways. It could be your parents. It could be your teachers.

As I keep saying (and hopefully you are listening), it's all about the people that really impacted your life between the ages of five and twelve.

The pattern you've seen is the pattern that you adopt.

Forgive

Okay, I know, I talked about forgiveness before. You're reading. That's good. But I'm going to keep talking about it. Over and over.

Why? Because forgiveness is key.

Forgiveness must be done by you and you alone.

We need to unload. And that's the work that we're doing. It's that discovery process.

It's figuring out, "Oh, my parents have a connection with that. Now I need to let go. I need to forgive them. It hurts because I love my parents, but now I realize that holding on to it didn't do me any favors. They made me who I am today, and because of that, I'm going to be that butterfly, and I'm going to forgive them. They must have also had a difficult life. And I don't know what their life was like."

For example, you may have been raised by parents who didn't know how to express love to you. This was because they didn't receive love themselves. Therefore, they didn't know what it meant to give love, and they repeated what they had learned.

If you cannot forgive, you won't be able to let go. You will remain attached to your shell and the place you are stuck in. You will never be able to fly away and be free. Or find that opportunity that was meant for you if you're still somehow attached to your past.

You have to forgive your parents because they didn't know what they were doing. They just raised you in the best way they knew how.

It's about you. It's about freeing yourself and believing your parents had no conscious part in it. They contributed to what you're feeling, but they didn't do it on purpose.

It's about freeing yourself by forgiving them without even having a conversation with them.

It's about writing unfiltered letters to your parents and the people who contributed to these patterns. Putting it on paper is freeing because you can express the pain you've been carrying. Write it down and get it out.

However, importantly, you can burn it or delete that file. You don't need to send it.

Just write.

You also write to your inner child because these patterns are your inner child expressing itself. So it's talking to your inner child and comforting them, and telling them it's going to be okay, and it's time to let go.

This is personal work. Forgiveness comes from the fact that you are who you are because of the pain you have gone through.

The best lesson I've learned about forgiveness is that I would not be who I am today if I didn't go through this pain and this life.

I would not be the resilient and strong person that I am.

I wouldn't be able to do what I do.

I wouldn't be able to figure out that I need to find myself and find my superpower, my gift.

That's what allows you to set yourself free and be the person you were meant to be.

That's the way to discover the path that you were meant to go along.

Let Go

It's time to let go of what was holding you back.

Now you can be free, and you can be in your full power.

You can now move forward and leave that place instead of staying where you falsely feel safe and comfortable.

When you get out of it, you are going to feel a sense of real safety.

In fact, it will redefine what safety means to you.

It doesn't mean cutting off your parents.

You let go because you forgive your parents and no longer hold a grudge against them.

You simply let go of what was holding you back.

Some people go back to their parents and talk to them. They have a conversation and tell them about the process they're going through, the work they're doing for themselves, and what they're discovering about themselves.

It could also be talking to your parents and understanding their past. Or it could just be having a different level of love.

Your love for your parents has shifted.

For example, maybe you had parents who were very absent and neglectful. When you visited them, you would just sit down and have non-loving conversations. Because you're hurt, and you've been carrying that grudge. You just say "hi" because you have respect for them.

You want to see how they're doing, but you don't enjoy it. You don't feel comfortable staying with them. You're just counting the time until you can leave that place. You're just doing your duty.

But now what you do is just go and hug them. That's a different interaction. You see them in a different light.

And if you're strong, you can also share your journey and what you've discovered, and see if they're going to receive it.

It will change how you interact with your parents because they will see that you've changed.

Now when you go and visit them, you have a different outlook. When you see them, you're different. It doesn't hurt anymore because they can't touch you.

You're free.

You receive their messages entirely differently.

When you talk to your parents with an attitude because you are hurt and react to what they say, you keep that link.

However, if you're free and don't have that link anymore, and they keep trying to hurt you, it's like throwing a rock that doesn't bounce back.

They may keep trying, but they don't get the same result. That feeling of discomfort is no longer there because you have that forgiveness.

You don't look at them the same way. You look at them from a loving place.

That's the difference, and that's why you don't feel the same pain.

When you've reached this point, you know you're free.

Redefine Safety

What should safety feel like?

Once you're set free, you don't want to go back. You have to be consistent in the work you're doing and the transformation that you're making.

You can't help but want to pursue safety because you're feeling better.

You're feeling lighter.

You're looking forward and not holding on to the past anymore.

Now you create new patterns and integrate them consistently into your life.

An example of a new pattern is expressing your needs. I can say, "I need love," or "I can choose myself first, instead of always sacrificing myself."

That's a new pattern. I automatically honor my needs first and take care of myself.

Every time I feel like I need something, I just go and work out.

I eat healthier.

I say, "No."

I surround myself with better people.

I engage with the community.

I don't avoid people.

I'm myself.

I replace my bad habits with good habits.

I create a process to generate that pattern. You change because this work leads you to doing that, and when you do it consistently, it becomes a habit.

You want to take care of yourself first. If you can't take care of yourself, how are you going to be able to take care of others?

At first, people who liked the old you may resent you. It's normal for human beings. When you sacrifice everything for others, most people take you for granted or disrespect them. They feel like they are entitled to what you do for them.

However, when they see you actually honoring your needs and being that amazing person, they respect it. So when you take care of yourself, you're strong and can help others.

You can kill yourself at work with 10,000 hours. But what happens when you're sick from working too much and sleeping too little?

Well, you can't work.

You're going to have to take sick days, and eventually, you may not be able to work at all.

Then you cannot pay your bills. You cannot support your family.

What about when you take care of yourself? You focus on staying healthy and balanced.

Taking care of yourself makes you feel good. You work out, feel great, and then come home feeling energized. You're full of endorphins, and you feel amazing.

You have a balanced life because you don't sacrifice your family and your time for work.

You still do great work. You're focused. You do what you need to do, but then you give time for yourself and your family.

Safe Flight

Okay, I've been walking you through a lot of things in this safety chapter. But most importantly, you want to fly safe.

What? Safe flying is basically the path to making a dent in the universe.

It's the path you're going to take to define your gift, to use it, leverage it, and make your mark.

Safe flight is that feeling of excitement for what's to come and having so much to do.

You get energized by the "new".

As you're discovering more about yourself and letting go of things holding you back, it creates a sense of creativity. It's energizing, and now you see possibilities.

You're curious, you want to explore more, and you want to do more.

You're feeling amazing, and you're healthier.

It's like adding ten years to your life.

You're flying, and you're free.

You're inspired.

You're curious.

There are so many attributes that we can talk about that define that sense of flight.

Safe flight leads to seeing new sights you've never seen before.

Remember that you were in a shell. It was dark. You were stuck, and you were confined. Your focus was not on what you wanted next. You kept hitting the shell in the same way. You were putting the energy in the wrong place.

But now that you see the light, you're free, lighter, and different.

You're flying.

Not only that, you're in a place where you're safely flying, and nothing is going to happen.

You're flying in the right direction and on the right path.

You're extremely clear about where you want to go and what you want to do. You're just going to continue focusing on that and moving forward.

That's the place of safety.

You're safer now because whatever the new choice or pattern you're creating is, it yields positive results.

You're not hurting yourself as much. You don't feel the same pain. You're completely changed.

Safety is a place where you feel completely yourself.

It's a place where it's safe to be you. You are free to be inspired, motivated, creative, and be the person you are meant to be.

Let's put it this way. If you don't find your launch

point, you will live a flat-line life and will die like many people who have gone through life without experiencing it to the fullest.

You haven't explored what you're capable of. You're leaving with your gift. You're burying it with you. You're not actually making a difference in this world.

Imagine if a million people did the same thing that you did. You're not helping this world. Also, if you have kids, you're essentially teaching them that that's what life is about.

Or ...

Imagine what the world would be like if everyone used the gift they were meant to have.

There would be so much love.

There would be so much creativity.

If you think you were born to just eat, work, sleep, and watch TV, then I'm sorry to say that's not what life is about. If you are just this little blob feeding itself, then all you are doing is wasting your life. You're not giving, and you're not contributing. Yet you complain every day that your life is not exciting.

Take action now! Change your life. Make an impact.

chapter six

Space

Before, you had a very narrow view of your world. It was limited to what you believed in and what you thought was true. You didn't see the possibilities because you just felt stuck. You were only looking inside and stayed in your shell.

You didn't know where you were going. It felt like there was no way out. You were suffocated. You didn't feel like there was anything for you.

But now the world is your oyster.

There are limitless possibilities and opportunities in front of you.

You have a full space to play with.

You don't feel like your life is boring anymore. You look at it in a new way. Your vision has expanded.

You have hope.

You look at things completely differently and realize that you can have access to anything you want. You're in a space where you know what you want.

Now you can see it's within reach. You can tap into these opportunities.

Job opportunities, entrepreneurial opportunities, travel opportunities, relationship opportunities, and much more. All these opportunities that you didn't know you had access to, are now right in front of you. It's just a matter of deciding which ones you want to tap into, and which ones are meant for you.

It's a sense of freedom.

It's a sense of power.

You're empowered now to choose where you want to go.

Your life used to be, "I go to work, do my job, then come home at night and play with my kids. Sometimes I take some vacation, sometimes not. I don't have time, and that's just the way it is.

"I feel like I'm not making any progress in my life. I get to see my kid grow, which is very important to me. I get to be with my family, and this is also very important to me, but I'm not fulfilled at work. I don't feel like I'm making any impact. I don't feel like I'm growing. I feel like I'm outgrowing the space I've built around myself. It's very uncomfortable."

It felt like there was no way out, and you needed help.

Fast-forward to the present. Now you are thinking, "I have unlimited possibilities. I love what I do. I built my own company. I'm my own boss.

"I'm not afraid to leave this unfulfilling job.

"I can go after a more exciting job.

"I can actually decide to buy the trailer of my dreams or travel around the world.

"I have a choice on how I want to live my life, how I want to use my gift, and what I want to do. It feels like I'm prolonging my life.

"I have many more choices than I thought I had, and it's exciting because those choices seem to be reachable.

"I can get them. I can touch them. I can use them."

Okay, you get the point. You're using different words, different language, and different ways of thinking about your life and work.

The walls of your belief no longer limit you. That's how it feels to have that vision of space.

This space is available to you, and it always has been.

You just decided subconsciously to put walls around yourself so that you couldn't access it.

I would like for you to attain this incredible epiphany that everything is possible and within your reach.

There's a purpose for you here, and it's exciting.

Within Reach

When you're building that false belief, that wall, you believe that's all you have access to. But getting rid of those false beliefs will make you realize that your dreams are possible and accessible.

Being in that shell made you ignore your aspirations and say, "I'm an imposter. I will never be able to succeed. I'm not important. I'm not good enough."

However, expanding your thoughts to your fullest potential will lead to the greatest breakthroughs and achievements.

You will think, "I didn't know it was that close. I didn't know I could switch careers. I didn't know that I could have access to these job opportunities.

"I didn't know I could build this company with

all the resources I had in front of me. I didn't know I was capable of doing it. I didn't know it was in me."

It's so inherent in you now that all of these things keeping you back are gone or manageable.

You feel so excited that you begin focusing on making it happen. And you actually make it happen.

That's the excitement of the vision. You can visualize that space now and the possibility of what you can do within it.

Now you can make it happen because you literally feel it. It's within your reach.

This is important because it gives your life purpose. Now your existence has meaning.

It's no longer gravitating around that feeling of "what it's supposed to be," like going through life like a flat line with no pulse.

You gave up on your dreams. You thought, "It doesn't matter what I love, I have to lead a responsible and safe life."

What you didn't realize was that by chasing your dreams, you would not only find joy, but you would also inspire your family to follow your lead. You would basically enable your family to dream with you and be excited with you.

So let's switch back to what you're doing now.

You're empowering people to do the same for themselves instead of being stuck in their own shells. You're leading them to see the possibilities.

You're inspiring them. And when you inspire people, you create followers. They follow you, and they're excited, and that gives you even more strength to do what you love.

It's not just about you. You have a ripple effect on all the people around you, especially your family and loved ones. And that feeling is what keeps you even more motivated.

In turn, you're no longer scared because you feel supported.

You've disrupted your old beliefs by being free, being in that openness, and being in that space where you have a place to make your own mark. To make an impact.

Now you have a positive mind, brimming with hope.

And you can spread hope to the people around you.

Way Out

There's a way out.

Actually, let's take that up a level.

Let's go beyond your comfort zone. You're going to stretch around the possibilities and feel more excited about accessing your talents and superpower.

Instead of saying, "I just thought I was good at this," or, "This is what I thought I was meant to do or be," the feeling of stretching yourself gives you a sense of power and of being more.

You thought you were only capable of doing certain things, and so many things were out of reach. But now you can see you're more than that.

You're more talented than you thought you were.

You have more strength than you thought you had. You can do many more exciting things that you didn't think you were capable of, or didn't think you had access to.

You're out of the shell.

We tend to hold ourselves back because we think we're not good enough, but all we need to do is tap into our core and realize our full potential to be great.

For many years, I thought I was not very smart because that's what I had been told repeatedly.

I came from a technology background and was a software engineer. I had access to every product, every concept, and every technology available at the time. And I would learn at the speed of light.

But I realized I was unhappy and just felt like I was stuck.

Looking back now, I realize that I was mentally limiting myself by saying that I was not very good at it and it was not important. I was learning, but I was not showing my best.

The only people I was showing my best to were my clients, but I couldn't do a good job internally. I was not growing because I was not showing that greatness. I locked it down.

So, when I was able to see all the strength I had, it was like poking a balloon and popping it. It was like unlocking something in my brain that was limiting my growth.

I discovered that I'm actually very smart and a fast learner. Not only that, I'm also very creative, and that creativity was exciting to me.

I had to unlock it and develop it.

First, I had to get rid of my shell, which I did.

I started developing more skills. I realized that I was good at human psychology and the human brain. I strengthened my intuition.

Before, I was not seen as a thought leader. I was not seen as a strategic person. I was seen as someone passionate about their clients and the product, but that's it.

It was the same feeling you might get if you were stuck in a confined space for many years, and forgot how to walk.

Therefore, I relearned how to walk, how to use my brain differently, how to stretch it, and therefore expand my potential. I did it through learning new skills, practicing, and having a coach. I found that I had opportunities to develop my leadership, strategy, and many other things that helped me accelerate my growth.

I obviously had that already in me. It was a part of my talents, I just had to develop them.

The more I learned and practiced, the more I increase my potential and got stronger.

I went up another level.

Eyes on the Opportunity

When you see the impact you're making, you don't want to stop.

The result is the people I have impacted in my life. I could see the positive impact I made on people. I witnessed their transformation.

My last career in corporate was the most amazing and rewarding experience I ever had as a leader. Not only was I able to use my skills to hire the best people, but it was the most amazing and talented team I've ever had the honor to lead.

For me, this was the direct result of my impact on the people and the company. When I saw that, I thought, "Okay, this was an amazing experience. Let's take it to another level. Let's expand outside of corporate."

I was expanding my potential.

Today, I feel incredibly blessed and grateful to do what I love and make a living doing it.

The testimonials are inspiring and keep me going. Now more than ever, I feel that I am making a positive and lasting impact in people's lives. I found my calling. It gives me more strength and energy to keep expanding it to whoever wants access to it.

That's what excites me.

Tap into Your Desire

We all need rewards. We all want to feel fulfilled. It's just human nature.

Do you want to live a life of significance?

Do you want a rewarding life?

Every time I ask a person what they would need in order to be fulfilled in life, they always say, "I need to be recognized. I need to be loved. I need to be important."

I rarely find someone who doesn't say that.

So I say, "Well, you have to first honor your needs and your talents." Because no matter what, we need that recognition. It's the reward. We all function with rewards.

It's like being addicted to something positive. You keep wanting more because you enjoy the feeling and the experience.

A reward could be someone coming to you and saying, "Thank you for changing my life forever. I found my purpose."

Or it could be the opportunities you create for others, which gives you more resources and freedom to keep growing yourself, and ultimately create the life you want.

For example, you could be passionate about sustainability, and now you have the opportunity to create a business. You find the people that you can collaborate with. You get the funding and resources you need to build your product or for your service to be successful.

In the past, you thought you couldn't do it because you were scared it would financially impact your family. But now you can see that you have access to the people who can help you. You can have resources that are within your reach.

Or maybe you're now the CIO of a small company that has an incredible culture. A culture that is empowering and inspiring to the people you lead. You didn't know you could do it before, but now you can be the leader you wanted to be and create a successful business.

After confidence comes clarity. Now the fears are gone, or are manageable. There will always be times when you have doubts, but now you know you can't return to that shell you were in.

Power of Choice

We have the power to make decisions.

When you're stuck, you don't think you have many choices. It's "either you do this, or you die." But when you realize that you actually have more options than you thought, dying is not even an option anymore. Now, compared to the original direction you thought was the only one, you have many more exciting choices.

That's the power of choice. It's knowing that you have more than two choices. Or, technically, one.

It makes you feel like you aren't stuck anymore. You can try things and see how they feel. And keep trying until you feel like you can expand. You're going to be exploring those opportunities in front of you to see if one of them is more exciting than the others.

However, having clarity is essential. You won't know what choice to make when you lack clarity. You're going to be anxious about making the wrong choice.

When you're confident, you accept failure as a learning experience.

Confidence says, "Sometimes I'm going to win, and sometimes I'm going to learn".

The fear of failure is what creates that anxiety and paralysis.

The power of choice is important if you want to keep moving forward in your life.

So, what do you want?

Do you want to feel like a failure, or do you want to feel like a success?

If you want your situation to change for the better, you've got to change the way you look at it.

Now that you're confident and clear, just list the opportunities you see in front of you. Pick the most exciting ones, but make a choice. Make an executive decision today and pursue it.

Remember that sometimes you will win, and sometimes you will learn.

But as long as you keep learning, you will keep moving forward.

That's the mindset that you want to keep having.

Never look back. Keep moving forward.

You can keep doing what you do and live the same boring life. But if you want to change your life, you have to change your thinking and focus. Where your focus goes, your energy flows.

Opportunities only become visible and accessible when you shift from a fixed mindset to a growth mindset.

These opportunities will create space for you. It takes work, but that work is energizing because you're excited about it.

There's a transition that will happen, but the excitement that you're getting by that transition is going to elevate the experience.

And eventually, you will switch and completely be in that new opportunity, in that new space.

There's a difference between loving what you're doing and being excited about what's coming, versus just doing it because you have no choice.

Most of us grew up that way. We thought, "This is what my life is going to look like." This doesn't allow us to cut into this other, bigger space that has actually been given to us at birth.

But there is hope.

That hope comes the day you realize you have access to that space. The day you recognize that, nothing will feel the same. You will never want to go back to your old life.

You're going to want to be in that new space, swimming in that ocean of opportunity and embracing the possibilities. And that strength you're getting, that stretching outside your comfort, is the most incredible feeling you'll ever feel in your life.

That feeling is getting rid of all the lies you've been hearing all your life about what your destiny is.

Take a leap.

Make an executive decision today to take on one of the choices you have in front of you.

It's okay.

Just play with it.

Have fun with it.

Your destiny is to make a dent in the universe.

Your destiny is to tap into that space, make it even better, and grow that space with other people.

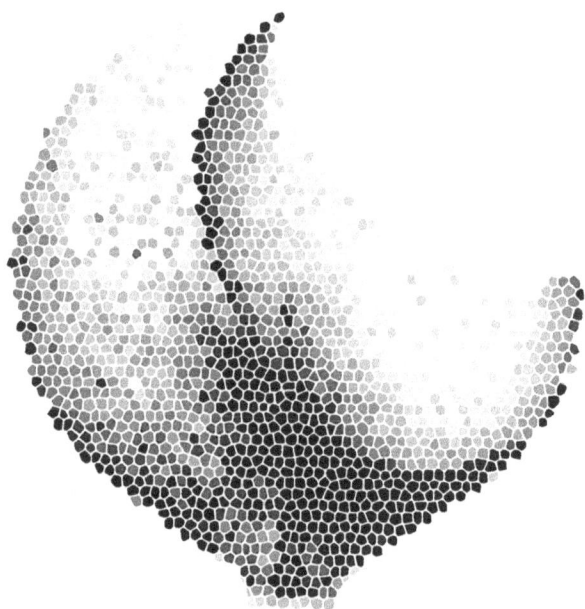

chapter seven

Spreading Joy

I firmly believe that our purpose is to guide and empower others with the gift of wisdom that experience has taught us.

By nurturing the growth and potential of those around us, we contribute to a ripple effect of positive change and the spreading of joy that extends far beyond our immediate sphere of influence.

You are equipped to spread joy and good words, and the fulfillment you experience should be shared with others. People can learn from you and benefit from your experiences.

By serving people and creating value for them, we can inspire them to do the same for others. Because there's always someone who needs help, especially with something that you went through. You were able to find a way, and now they need that way.

Let's talk about unconditional joy.

Like a father coming home after a long day to see the smiles on his kids' faces.

It's a sense of freedom, the cherry on top, that represents unadulterated happiness, the kind that knows no bounds.

You've found yourself and finally freed yourself from that shell.

You've found your gift, and you're finally using it.

Not only that, but you're using it with joy because you're no longer the person you were before you started this process.

You're a completely brand-new person with stronger wings, energy, and fulfillment. It's similar to an uncontrollable laughter that simply cannot be contained.

You are no longer bound to the darkness and sadness that once held you captive.

The place where you were stuck is now in the past.

There are so many possibilities that lie ahead of you.

You're free.

You're lighter.

Who wouldn't want such liberation and the joy that comes with it?

The shadows of the past have left you, making room for an overwhelming desire for you to share the good news.

There's no other way because this joy is contagious.

Excitement surges within you because you have discovered your purpose and found your true joy.

There is an inner call, a sense of urgency to spread this revelation that you know people around you need to hear. People that can see your transformation and need to hear your compelling message.

As human beings, when we finally pass through the transformation process, the instinct to share it with others takes over. It's like bursting with thrilling news, and you want others to partake in that feeling of exhilaration.

Sometimes, people around you notice that shift in your demeanor and ask what's going on. You say, "I have to share it with you! This is what's happening in my life!"

When someone notices that positive change in us, it's hard to contain our excitement. The natural impulse is to share it.

Once we reach that elevated stage of euphoria, spreading joy becomes an integral part of our being. It becomes innate and we want more people to bask in the same boundless state of joy.

When you reach that state, you cannot help but

want to share it and spread the news. It's just who we are. We want more people with us. We want more people to experience that feeling. It's like offering someone a taste of delicious ice cream and insisting they try it too.

Our ability to connect with others often determines the process of sharing joy. While some individuals, particularly introverts or those with certain beliefs, may hesitate to reach out, you have to do it. The act of connecting becomes an essential part of sharing your gift because it ignites a chain reaction of joy.

When we feel elated, our expressions, be it through words or body language, draw curious glances from others. We essentially become walking beacons of happiness, spreading light and joy even without consciously doing so.

A simple smile, for example, is a universal response to the warmth of joy you feel within you. It's also a language understood by all.

People can't help but notice a radiant glow and ask you, "What's your secret?" Or perhaps, our own euphoria overwhelms us, and we enthusiastically share the source of our bliss, encouraging them to experience it too.

In my work with clients, I often witness this phenomenon. When they reach a state of pure bliss, they can't help but express it. They feel compelled to talk about their newfound feelings of wonder.

My goal is to guide them out of their shells and into a place of self-discovery, where they can embrace their talents and share them with the world. I believe that we are not meant to keep our gift for ourselves. I think that someone, somewhere, needs our message. Growth and progress stem from knowledge that is freely passed on from one person to another.

The exchange of knowledge and gifts paves the way for collective growth and achievement.

It's a simple truth.

All the knowledge we possess is because someone chose to share it. Without knowledge sharing, we wouldn't have data, and we wouldn't know what we know. The very existence of AI relies on data that has been shared. Our ability to gather and use knowledge to accomplish tasks depends on the willingness of others to share their expertise.

Think about it. If no one had shared with me how to build a house, how would I ever know how to do it? Our progress as human beings is indebted to the act of sharing knowledge and gifts. It's a fundamental aspect of our existence.

Growing up with an unhappy father who was burdened by the choices he made significantly impacted me. It influenced my career decisions, and I picked jobs not for joy, but out of necessity.

I had to work. I found myself following a path similar to my father's, prioritizing family but lacking personal fulfillment in my work.

He was only ever happy when he was with us, but he was stuck behind a desk doing something he didn't enjoy for the rest of his day.

Observing my father's struggle is how I realized that I was called to help people find joy in their lives.

And the only way I could help them do that was

to help them discover themselves and to get them out of their shell, so they could find their gift. I have a unique ability to mirror back peoples' gifts and talents. That's my "why," the purpose that drives me.

As a daughter, I experienced this firsthand and eventually unraveled the truth. I knew then that I had to share this revelation with the world. Helping others became my mission, driven by the knowledge that life shouldn't be lived without it. It's about breaking free from the cycle of unhappiness because there's no fulfillment in living such a life.

I don't believe living a monotonous nine-to-five life behind a desk is our true purpose.

It's a cycle we repeat because we see our parents doing it to provide for the family. We feel it's the way to go, but deep down, it's not fulfilling.

Though I was successful in my career, I realized my success came from my ability to connect with people and learn quickly. Despite this, I felt like I was missing out on what I was called to do. However, at that time, I didn't know what it was until I figured it out in the process.

When I look at the evolution of the world, I'm convinced that without individuals daring to follow their callings, we would not be where we are today. We would not be here, and human progress would grind to a halt.

Things started to click for me. I felt a sense of responsibility to do my part, to make a meaningful contribution to the world.

Seeing my dad's misery and recalling my own experiences, I felt a calling to help others stuck in the same situation because I have been there.

I missed six months of my son's life that I will never get back. Although six months may seem insignificant, it meant a great deal to me.

Even after returning to a regular schedule, I continued to work extensively. And for what? Simply for a paycheck.

I wouldn't wish this on anyone because, in my experience, I haven't met anyone who finds joy in just sitting at their desk, doing a job they don't love.

It's such a waste of a gift.

The path to finding this gift lies in understanding ourselves, our strengths, needs, values, and beliefs. These tools enable introspection and are the very ones I use to guide others on their journey of self-discovery.

Be Naked

I expect my clients to be vulnerable and open.

It's the same thing with my readers. You cannot start the process unless you're vulnerable.

You need to be able to shed protective layers and embrace vulnerability. If you continue holding back, clinging to the past, and never letting go, this process will never work.

Being vulnerable is crucial. While most who come to me are willing to be vulnerable, some will still grapple with reservations, such as the fear of hurting loved ones, with sentiments like, "I don't want to hurt my parents." However, openness and willingness to share are essential to letting go of the barriers that impede progress.

Without vulnerability, you'll slow down the process, and the experience lacks its full potential. Remaining closed off prolongs the time spent in your shell, hindering personal progress.

Vulnerability is the first step of growth.

Vulnerability is an emotional experience. Opening up a part of your life to share is like exposing an open wound. It feels sensitive and raw. However, there's a sense of release and relief in that pain as you let go.

Being vulnerable brings forth a range of emotions. You may feel angry, sad, or moved to tears. This sensitivity makes you feel naked, but the outcome is truly amazing.

Next, recognize that openness is important to the process. If you give half of the story, you're hindering your own progress.

Use the Gift

Discovering and using your gifts feels like you finally found yourself.

When you fully embrace your true self and unleash your gift, you experience newfound freedom and incredible fulfillment. Instead of feeling burdened by your daily routine, using your gift fills you with boundless energy. You naturally produce excellent results because you genuinely enjoy what you're doing. That's the gift.

Your gift is your passion. It's the superpower we talked about earlier in the book. It is the thing that you love doing, excel at, and can immerse yourself in for hours.

One of my clients, a corporate business executive raised in a military family, faced high expectations. He was discouraged from pursuing art as a career because he was told it wasn't financially viable. Consequently, he chose the path of business but always felt a void in his heart.

Eventually, he carved out a space in his home to indulge his passion for painting. It quickly became a source of immense joy for him, and he realized that he had to make it part of his life, even if there was a process to get there.

Moreover, he now wishes to share this liberating experience with others, especially with men who have had to suppress their artistic talents, perhaps due to frustration from being told they can't make a living out of it.

He now has a clear goal: to open a gallery, art school, or some art-related venture where he can share his gift with those who have suppressed their artistic talents. Financing this endeavor is his current mission.

Through coaching, he found his freedom. He once believed he had to retrain himself to pursue art, but now he knows it's unnecessary. Now he gets a lot of joy just painting in his basement, having that outlet to express his art, and eventually share it with others.

It's excitement and joy, and he's ready to spread it.

Spread the News

There is a burning desire to share your life-changing transformation with others, because you want to give that knowledge or experience to people struggling with the same things you care about. You want to be able to show the process you went through, why you feel so amazing, and what you're doing now.

Personally, I wake up every day feeling joyful.

My secret, which I want to share with everyone, is to disconnect from social media and the news. By living life to the fullest without constant noise exposure, you can find happiness every day.

I'm still content even when I'm not feeling my best or have a headache. Being alive and engaging in activities I love, like meeting with clients, brings a genuine sense of happiness that outweighs my temporary discomfort.

While it's true that losing someone and getting hurt may bring sadness, humans are resilient creatures. There are countless individuals who, despite facing heart-wrenching tragedies like losing their loved ones or families, still wake up with the determination to push forward.

I won't say there are no exceptions to this, but usually, when you go through this process of transformation, you acquire effective stress management tools, and you bounce back stronger.

Despite facing uncontrollable circumstances, the ability to keep moving forward and finding strength in resilience is a powerful force.

If you witness someone laughing heartily on the floor, you can't help but laugh too. It's contagious. Test it. Observe someone genuinely laughing, and you'll find yourself smiling automatically.

Wouldn't you prefer to be around someone inspiring and happy rather than someone feeling down? Being in the company of joyful and inspiring individuals feels great and more fulfilling.

Spreading joy affects how you feel and enables you to share that feeling with others.

Similar to sunflowers turning toward the sun, humans seek that light.

Even for individuals facing clinical depression and requiring medication, experiencing joy remains a crucial emotion for human well-being. It is a vital emotion because it brings happiness and good health.

When you feel joy, the whole of you is happy.

It's going to show even without you saying a word. Whether you express it or people ask you about it, you spread the good news.

Joy is the ultimate feeling that all humans should aspire to experience.

Choose

I realized that I was a happy child, and my family members often told me, "You were always a happy little girl."

However, I couldn't understand why they said that because I didn't have any fond memories that made me happy. My upbringing and relationships weren't the best. But now I realize how happy I was, and I realize that I had that inner joy within me.

This realization made the process of finding myself easier. I understood that I had lost my sunshine in that last relationship that I had, and I couldn't stay in that mental state forever.

I needed to find my joy again because that person is not who I am. When I reached the end of my self-discovery, I discovered true joy and decided to keep moving forward.

Approaching the two-year mark before leaving my corporate job, my happiness, and excitement kept growing. I consciously decided to disconnect from negative noise as it did not bring me joy. It was then that I experienced the ultimate feeling of happiness.

The process is for everyone. As human beings, we naturally experience a wide range of emotions, including joy and tears. We can laugh, we can cry, we have the capacity for both.

Even if someone had an unhappy childhood, it doesn't mean they cannot find joy.

Joy can be discovered by actively seeking it. Observing someone smile often triggers a positive response in us, making us smile in return. I find it hard to believe you will not smile when you see someone smiling.

I've seen so many sad kids, and when you try to

make them laugh, they start laughing, and then they forget they were sad. It's the same for us.

We can always transform sadness into joy because we experience a full range of emotions. By making changes to our lives and circumstances, we can express all of these emotions. It all starts with choosing to embrace change.

We may not always have control over our circumstances, but we can always choose how we respond to them. Even in the face of difficult situations, we have the power to change our outlook and make a choice to bounce back.

For example, if we experience the loss of a loved one, we cannot control that event, but we can choose how we rebound from the grief. Similarly, if we lose our job and find ourselves in a tough spot, we can still decide to rise above the challenge and find a way to move forward.

There's always a way.

There are countless success stories of how people have turned their lives around despite difficult circumstances, even if they went to prison. Many individuals have faced jail time but decided to make a change upon release instead of thinking there was no hope for them or that society would no longer accept them and returning to their old ways. They chose a different path and transformed their lives.

You can do anything you want.

Anyone can turn their life around if they choose to.

We can't control the events, but we can choose how we adapt and how we change our lives. That's a fact. It's a choice.

Life is about choices. You can let yourself go and accept the life you have, or you can change it and have a better life. The power to choose is in your hands.

You can choose to spread joy.

You can choose to turn your life around, to make a difference. You can choose all that.

Whatever I'm teaching you, pass it on to someone else in need. Share your newfound knowledge and gift with others who can benefit from it.

When you're truly happy with yourself and feel amazing in your skin, you cannot help but share it. That joy will naturally radiate, and you'll inspire those around you. Embrace your nature to share and uplift others, whether through words or your glowing presence.

This entire journey has been about choices.

You can either live a miserable life and keep your gift hidden, or you can create an incredible life, share your gift, and leave a lasting legacy.

The choice is yours to make an impact and leave your mark.

If your finance job is merely about helping a corporation stay afloat, it may not be fulfilling. However, if it involves helping people find their wealth and design the life of their dreams, then it becomes a meaningful gift to share.

If you find yourself going to an office job feeling miserable, longing for a life filled with passion, but feeling like you don't have the power to change, then I'm sad for you.

You have two options: You can choose a life of misery and stagnation, leading to a pointless existence. You're like a walking dead man.

But there's another choice: You can transform your life, embrace your gift, and lead an extraordinary and fulfilling existence.

You not only get to enjoy your gift, but you also leave a lasting legacy, a mark with your name on it. A legacy that touches people's lives forever.

You have the power to leave an incredible mark on this world, something that will endure through the years and generations, carrying your name forward.

The choice is entirely yours. I sincerely hope you choose happiness.

I hope as you read this, you will wake up and make the choice to be happy and filled with purpose, and then go out and spread it.

The more people we can change in this world, the better the world will be.

Indeed, we need a better world filled with more joy that will send a ripple effect.

People are yearning for this, especially in these times, and we are naturally born with the ability to give and receive it. If everyone is willing to share this precious gift, this planet we live on will be a paradise.

We'll do better things for the planet Earth. We will take better care of it because we need nature, and nature needs us.

We'll have less illness, and people will live longer and healthier.

Life is unpredictable, and we shouldn't wait for it to knock us down before starting the process of change.

Tomorrow is uncertain, but what is certain is that we possess the ability to design our lives according to our desires.

Find your gift, put in the work, and share it with the world.

It is a gift that keeps on giving. Doing this will bring you joy that you can spread to others around you so they can experience that same transformative power.

We need each other to create this beautiful change.

Conclusion

We have only one life.

You might have a different belief. If you believe in reincarnation, good for you. But at the end of the day, whether you believe in reincarnation or not, we have one life.

And this life has been given to us so we can do something with it.

To build something.

To make an imprint.

To leave a legacy.

So if we're just born and take it, and let our circumstances determine our lives, then we'll be wasting it.

I am the daughter of a man who sacrificed his dreams to build a family. Looking back, I realize my father was stuck in a marriage that was probably not the best for him.

However, he made a choice. He put his wife and us first, making me realize we are here for a reason.

Today, my dad has dementia. He's sick, and although he's 80 years old, he looks 100. He looks beaten down because he's never really experienced life and love in the way he probably wanted to.

The reason I'm writing this book is because I don't want you to be my dad or be regretful about your life.

I don't want you to be one of those people who were just born and never use that gift. Someone who isn't maximizing this blessing because life has been hard on you.

There are so many people who have very hard lives, but they've overcome their challenges and made something of it. There are people born without arms and legs, but they made a difference. There are products and services for disabled people because of those incredible souls that decided not to let life beat them up.

So why not you? You have the same ability.

Leave all this crap holding you back.

Let go of all things that are not serving you and are causing you more trouble.

Do something magical with your life.

Do something beautiful.

Make something that not only you are proud of, but if you have people that you will leave this to, they would be proud to carry it on for you for the rest of humanity.

This is not a plea. It's a wake-up call.

It doesn't matter how old you are. If you are mentally capable, and in relatively good health, then just do something.

Nora Paxton

Make a change.

Take charge and believe it's possible.

You've got to make a difference, not only in your life, but in the life of the people you impact.

I know it's going to be a long road because you can't just switch it on like a light, but you can change your life for the better if you follow the process. You will not only create this fulfillment, but also inspire your children and the future generations behind you to do the same.

It sounds daunting and impossible because of what has been put in your head. Things like, "It's too hard," "I am not good enough, smart enough, strong enough," and, "Life is about just having kids and raising them, ensuring their safety and security, moving on, and then enjoying life."

I wish you could see life differently because you've been blessed with such an incredible gift, but you chose to keep it for the people you love and not share it.

And now you're showing the same thing to your kids. You're teaching them that this is what life is about.

But your kids also have an incredible gift that they need to figure out and share with this world. A gift that will help them pursue a fulfilling life and positively impact other people.

We are all resilient.

We don't know how many days we have on this earth, but we do know that all of us have inherited a gift.

It's built into us. We just have to tap into it and say, "You know what? Life is throwing rocks at me, but I'm going to build a shield. I'm going to keep moving forward, and I'm going to put my stamp where it should be."

If you are someone who has suffered a lot from your childhood and overcame it, you have a story. You have a message for someone who needs it, somewhere in this world. Why don't you show them how to get away from it?

Your message is meant for someone else on this earth. You would be the best example that someone can look at.

Someone, somewhere, needs you.

We need you.

You're a piece of the puzzle.

Our time is limited, so let's make the most of it. We'll make this world a better place if we're all in this together. We'll be better humans as a result.

We'll inspire others to follow us.

And it only takes one person to get started.

So let's begin.

I want to invite you to do that. We may not have power over what's going on in the world, but we have the power within us to change what's in front of us.

Let's go through that transformation and make a difference.

Don't let your gift go to waste.

I will fight because I can't let you die like this.

It makes me sad for you. It makes me sad for the generation behind you. It makes me sad for your children, who are potentially following your lead because that's all you're modeling.

It makes me sad for all the people who are missing out on the gift that you have. The gift you could share that could totally transform their lives.

Get out of your comfort zone right now and decide, "Today is the first day of my new life, and I will never stop until I get where I need to be."

If I hadn't made that decision, I would probably

be stuck doing a 9 to 5 unfulfilling job or living paycheck to paycheck. Or maybe I'd be on the street begging for money and food if I didn't believe in myself enough because I let my circumstances and parents negatively impact my life. I could have done that, but I chose to reframe my perspective because it helped me build resilience and strength that made me who I am.

And today, I've had an incredible impact on the lives of so many men and women. My clients' children, employers, and the people around them are benefiting. Their lives have been changed forever, and they don't want to go back. They're making so many amazing, incredible dents in the universe that will remain for centuries because of the work they've done for themselves.

I changed because I didn't want to be a mental and physical abuse victim. I changed because I didn't want to be the saddest person. I changed because I wanted to show that I could completely decide my future.

I made that decision with my free will and said, "I want to make a difference. I want to change my life. But I can only do it by changing myself. By working on myself. By rebuilding myself in a very healthy way."

And I eventually did it. It took me many years, but I never gave up. Here I am, writing this book today.

You're the master of your choices, and you can still choose.

It's up to you.

About the Author

Nora Paxton is an executive coach who has dedicated herself to working with leaders to create meaning in their own lives and organizations. She brings over 25 years of experience in corporate and technology sectors to her clients, including leadership of high-performance teams.

Nora's compassionate and results-oriented work with her clients drives towards the outcomes of motivated employees, customer commitment, and bottom-line performance, as well as personal and professional balance and success.

She lives and works in Washington.

Find out more at norapaxton.com

www.ingramcontent.com/pod-product-compliance
Lightning Source LLC
Chambersburg PA
CBHW041144230326
41599CB00039BA/7173